I0820426

First published in the UK by Sona Books, an imprint of Danann Media Publishing Limited

CAT NO. SON0641

Written by

Dr Nyri A Bakkalian
Hareth Al Bustani
Alice Barnes-Brown
Aiden Dalby
Marc DeSantis
Alicea Francis
Ben Gazur
Bee Ginger
Charles Ginger
Jack Griffiths
April Madden

Proof reader: Cameron Thurlow

Images courtesy of

Alamy
Getty Images
Helen Field
National Land Image Information
Ministry of Land, Infrastructure, Transport and Tourism
Rogers Fund
1922/CC0 1.0
Bourrichon/CC BY-SA 2.0
PHGCOM/CC BY-SA 3.0
663highland/CC BY-SA 3.0
wikiwikiyarou/CC BY-SA 3.0
Integrated Collections Database of the National Museums
Japan/CC BY 4.0
Ministry of Foreign Affairs of Japan/CC BY 4.0
Artanisen/CC BY-SA 4.0
wiki/Rc 13/ CC BY-SA 4.0
wiki/Wiiii/CC BY-SA 3.0
wiki/663highland/CC BY-SA 3.0
wiki/内閣府ホームページ/CC BY 4.0
wiki/人事院ホームページ/CC BY 4.0
wiki/Bernard Gagnon/CC BY-SA 3.0
wiki/Suicasmo/CC BY-SA 4.0
wiki/663highland/CC BY-SA 3.0
Naokijp/CC BY-SA 4.0
しんぎんぐきゃっと/CC BY-SA 4.0
黄檗研究/ CC BY-SA 4.0
法雲寺/CC BY-SA 3.0
掬茶/CC BY-SA 3.0 (Sogo)
ElHeineken/CC BY 4.0
wiki/Archive.org
wiki/ Fujiwara No Takanobu
wiki/David Luizo
wiki/Asahi Shinbun-sha
wiki/Kikuchi Yosai
wiki/Marco
wiki/Tsukioka Yoshitoshi
wiki/Yoshitoshi
wiki/Utagawa Toyonobu
wiki/cha.go.kr
wiki/ morimiya.net
wiki/retabloceramico.net
wiki/Hokusai
wiki/Joe Rosenthal
Sailko/CC BY-SA 3.0
Sony Pictures Television/Courtesy Everett Collection/Alamy
The Asahi Shimbun/Getty Images

Made in EU.

ISBN: 978-1-917259-14-9

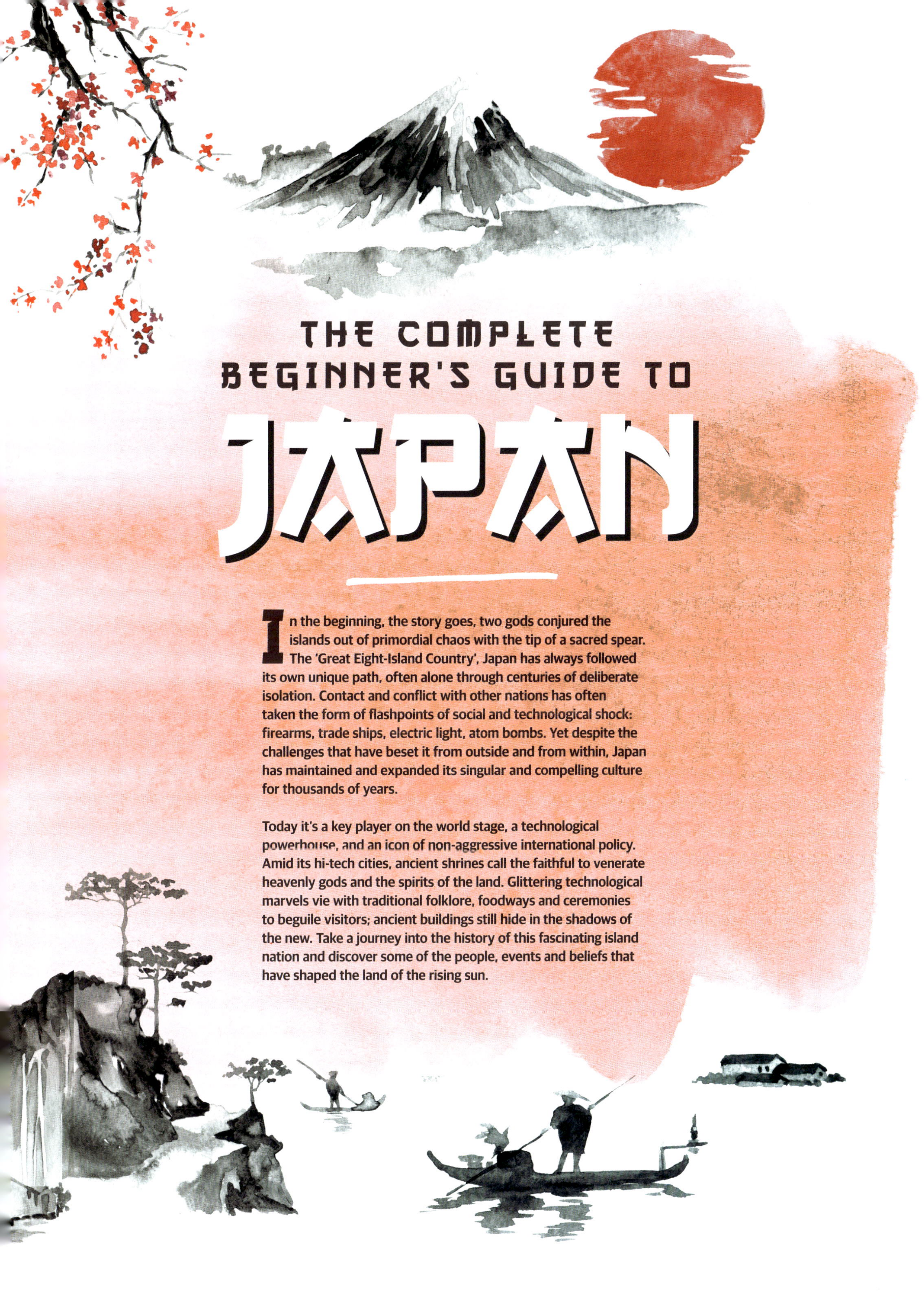

THE COMPLETE BEGINNER'S GUIDE TO JAPAN

In the beginning, the story goes, two gods conjured the islands out of primordial chaos with the tip of a sacred spear. The 'Great Eight-Island Country', Japan has always followed its own unique path, often alone through centuries of deliberate isolation. Contact and conflict with other nations has often taken the form of flashpoints of social and technological shock: firearms, trade ships, electric light, atom bombs. Yet despite the challenges that have beset it from outside and from within, Japan has maintained and expanded its singular and compelling culture for thousands of years.

Today it's a key player on the world stage, a technological powerhouse, and an icon of non-aggressive international policy. Amid its hi-tech cities, ancient shrines call the faithful to venerate heavenly gods and the spirits of the land. Glittering technological marvels vie with traditional folklore, foodways and ceremonies to beguile visitors; ancient buildings still hide in the shadows of the new. Take a journey into the history of this fascinating island nation and discover some of the people, events and beliefs that have shaped the land of the rising sun.

CONTENTS

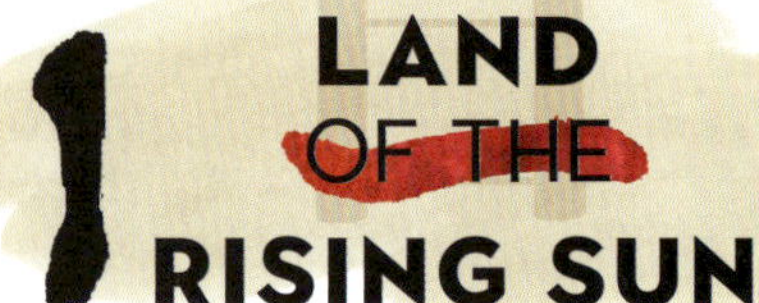

1 LAND OF THE RISING SUN

2 THE SHOGUN & THE SAMURAI

3 RESTORATION & REVOLUTION

CONTENTS

日出ずる国

LAND OF THE RISING SUN

ANCIENT ISLANDS WAR
LAND OF EIGHT MILLION GODS
KINGDOM LINES ARE DRAWN

PERIODS & ERAS

JOMON PERIOD
C. 10500 BCE

From what evidence exists, we know that the people at the time use tools and jewellery that are complex for their time. These are made from antlers, bones and stone. Rice cultivation dates back to this time too.

NARA PERIOD
710

Empress Genmei establishes Japan's first capital in Nara in 710. It later moves to Nagaoka in 784 and then to Kyoto in 794, where it would remain for over 1000 years. The Imperial Court creates the Kojiko and Nihon Shoki, chronicling Japan's history.

DID YOU KNOW?
Todai-ji, constructed in Nara in 738, houses the world's largest bronze buddha

DID YOU KNOW?
In 1713, Tokugawa Ietsugu became the youngest shogun ever at age four

KAMAKURA PERIOD
1185

The first shogun, Minamoto no Yoritomo, is appointed and he creates a new government that becomes known as the shogunate. The samurai emerge as a power that leads to feudalism. During this period, the Mongols attempt to invade Japan twice and fail.

YAYOI PERIOD
C. 300 BCE

The first signs of clans emerge. People start using metals like iron and bronze, build villages, adopt farming practices, and develop sophisticated agricultural techniques.

NANBOKU-CHŌ PERIOD (NORTHERN COURT)
1336

Based in Kyoto, the Northern Court eventually wins the conflict with the Southern Court in 1392. Today's imperial family are descended from the Northern Emperor.

10500 BCE — 300 BCE — 250 CE — 538 — 710 — 794 — 1185 — 1336

KOFUN PERIOD
C. 250 CE

Named after the tombs that were built for the rulers at the time, the Kofun period marks the first time Japan is unified under one leader.

ASUKA PERIOD
538

Buddhism is introduced to the country and adopted by the Imperial family, significantly changing the country's culture. The written language is adopted from Korea and China.

NANBOKU-CHŌ PERIOD (SOUTHERN COURT)
1336

The country is split into two imperial courts, Northern and Southern, after the Kenmu Restoration is overthrown. Emperor Go-Daigo establishes the Southern Court in Yoshino.

HEIAN PERIOD
794

The country sees a period of peace. Arts, literature and culture thrive as the Japanese scripts katakana and hiragana come to use, replacing Chinese as the official written language. The Fujiwara clan reigns throughout the majority of this time.

MUROMACHI PERIOD
1336

The government's power and influence begins to fade. Various samurai warlords and clans rise in power and wage civil war for decades.

MEIJI ERA
1868
Emperor Meiji moves the capital to Tokyo and begins the Meiji Restoration, ending the shogunate and reinstating imperial rule. A stagnant Japan is hundreds of years behind other countries, and so it opens its borders and rapidly modernises.

REIWA ERA 2019
Emperor Akihito abdicates the throne, the first emperor to do so in two centuries. Naruhito becomes the new emperor but the covid pandemic limits his public appearances.

SENGOKU PERIOD
1467
Known as the 'Warring States Period,' the daimyo (feudal lords) wage war against each other over control of land.

DID YOU KNOW?
Emperor Meiji was 15 years old when he ascended to the imperial throne

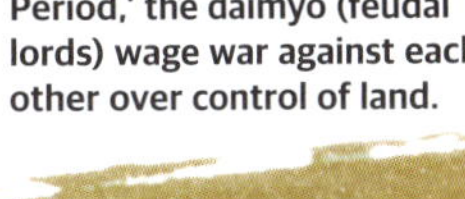

AZUCHI MOMOYAMA PERIOD 1568
Oda Nobunaga begins to unify Japan before he is betrayed and killed by Akechi Mitsuhide. Japan's largest castle, Himeji Castle, is heavily remodelled during this period.

SHŌWA ERA (POST-WAR) 1945
After the US drops atomic bombs on Hiroshima and Nagasaki, Japan surrenders and as part of the surrender, the Allied Powers occupy the country.

1467 — 1573 — 1603 — 1868 — 1912 — 1926 — 1945 — 1989 — 2019

EDO PERIOD
1603
Emperor Go-Yozei appoints Tokugawa Ieyasu as shogun, who establishes a government in Edo. In 1635, the Tokugawa shogunate bans Japanese citizens from leaving the country and stops anyone from entering, while trade with foreigners is restricted.

TAISHŌ ERA
1912
Japan joins the Allied powers during World War I, fighting German forces in East Asia and joins the League of Nations after the war.

SHŌWA ERA (PRE-WAR) 1926
Japan begins a war with China, invading Manchuria and committing war atrocities before aligning with Germany in the Second World War.

HEISEI ERA 1989
Japan's rapid economic growth in the 80s comes to an abrupt end in the 1990s. Amid numerous natural disasters and political instability, Japan experiences a cultural boom with the 'Cool Japan' movement, with anime and video games culture soaring in popularity.

GOD EMPERORS & WARRIOR QUEENS

THE EARLIEST HISTORY OF JAPAN IS SHROUDED IN MYTHS AND LEGENDS OF EMPERORS DESCENDED FROM GODS AND QUEENS WHO WAGED BLOODY WARS

The human history of Japan dates back at least 30,000 years. At that point, the four main islands of Japan were connected and land bridges joined them to both Korea in the south and Siberia in the north. The first humans to occupy what is now Japan simply walked in.

While their stories remain in the archaeological record as flint tools and the remnants of settlements, we know almost nothing of their history. The development of writing tells us what the Japanese said about themselves. What little does emerge may be part-myth and part-truth, but it reveals a society often riven by war.

THE JŌMON & THE YAYOI

The first culture to develop in Japan was the Jōmon around 10,000 BCE. We do not know what the Jōmon called themselves, but their name comes from their distinctive pottery style of intricately arranged cords, which archaeologists call Jōmon, meaning rope-patterned. Some of the pottery created by the later Jōmon would not look out of place in a modern art gallery. Their stylised pottery statues of people known as dogū so closely resemble spacemen in suits that some take them to be evidence of alien contact.

LEFT The Soga clan and then the Fujiwara clan came to dominate the royal court through marriage of their daughters into the imperial family

Contact with space aliens is unlikely, but when contact came between Japan and Asia it spelled the doom of the Jōmon people. Climate change around 1000 BCE saw them driven further south in Japan by cold weather. The Yayoi of China lived in a lush environment that dried out around the same time to create the Gobi desert of today. This destruction of their homelands caused a wave of migration. At first settling in Korea, the Yayoi then began migrating to Japan around 300 BCE. With their arrival, 10,000 years of Jōmon culture disappeared from the archaeological record.

Not much is known about the displacement of the Jōmon. Was it in a single wave of migration? Were they destroyed by warfare? The alternative is that the Yayoi came in smaller numbers over a long period and integrated themselves.

Recent analysis of DNA has revealed that on average, a modern Japanese person derives only around ten per cent of their genes from the Jōmon. However the Yayoi came to Japan, their offspring swamped those of the Jōmon. The indigenous Ainu of Japan share more DNA with the Jōmon though, so it is possible some aspects of Jōmon culture survived in them.

Because of their lack of a writing system, our knowledge of Yayoi culture is limited. We do know that they formed clans called uji. At the head of each clan stood a man who mediated between humans and spirits, or kami, as well as acting as a military leader. Over times these clans grew in power and territorial size, forming the first states in Japan.

LEFT The first emperor of Japan was the legendary Jimmu, who led his people eastward and conquered other kings – with the aid of a three-legged crow

ABOVE The first emperor of Japan, Jimmu, is said to have been descended from the gods and created the imperial throne through conquest

The Yayoi brought crucial innovations to Japan. The cultivation of rice emerged at the same time as the Yayoi arrived. The stone tools of the Jōmon were abandoned in favour of metal implements that allowed greater working of the land. Weapons and armour of bronze and iron reached Japan around the same time, mostly imported from China or Korea because of the lack of metal ores in Japan. By the 1st century CE, axe heads, spears and swords made of iron were becoming common throughout Japan. Conflict between clans drove the need for ever more weaponry.

THE FIRST EMPEROR

According to the two great works of Japanese legend written in the 8th century CE, the Kojiki and Nihon Shoki, the first emperor of Japan was Jimmu. Born in 711 BCE, Jimmu was a descendant of the goddess Amaterasu and, with his brothers, was the leader of a clan. They sought a location to cement their rule. "By dwelling in what place shall we most quietly carry on the government of the empire? It were probably best to go east."

Together they led their people east. Jimmu was provided with a sword that was magically sent by a deity to use in battle. As they travelled east, they fought a clan under the command of Nagasunehiko - the long-legged man - and were defeated. Jimmu realised that because they were fighting eastwards, they were fighting against the rising of the sun and so approached from the east, under the guidance of an eight-foot-long crow. This time Jimmu was victorious and settled the land of Yamato. We are told that he "extirpated the unsubmissive people".

"PEACE WAS RESTORED BUT DID NOT LONG SURVIVE HIMIKO'S DEATH"

Other clan leaders accepted the right of Jimmu to rule, thus marking his accession as monarch of Japan. Alongside other improbable facts, we are told that Jimmu lived to the age of 126. The chronicles that set down the life of Jimmu were written over 1,000 years after his supposed rule. Many consider Jimmu to be wholly legendary, but some wonder whether the tale of his migration might have echoes of the coming of the Yayoi people to Japan.

THE CIVIL WARS OF WA & QUEEN HIMIKO

Much of Japanese history at this early date is conjectural and little can be known for sure. Early Chinese accounts of their interactions with the Japanese, who they called Wa, record the trade of iron weapons and also the reasons they may have been required.

According to Chinese sources: "During the reigns of Huandi [147-168 CE] and Lingdi [168-189 CE] the country of Wa was in a state of great confusion, war and conflict raging on all sides. For a number of years, there was no ruler. Then a woman named Himiko appeared. Remaining unmarried, she occupied herself with magic and sorcery and bewitched the populace. Thereupon they placed her on the throne." This civil war of the Wa is the earliest historical war in Japan of which we have a written record, but much remains mysterious.

Himiko is said to have been a shaman and queen of Yamatai, whose location remains unknown. We are told she lived in a palace

ABOVE Empress Kōken abdicated but continued to influence behind the scenes - until she retook the throne with the monk Dōkyō by her side

surrounded by ever-vigilant guards. She had 1,000 female attendants, but only one man who relayed her orders. Apparently Himiko was a great ruler and brought peace to her kingdom. She sent emissaries to the Chinese court and received praise in return.

Himiko did not pacify all of Japan, however, and Himikuko, ruler of a rival state, rose in conflict against her. Peace was restored but did not long survive Himiko's death. "Then a king was placed on the throne, but the people would not obey him. Assassination and murder followed; more than 1,000 were thus slain. A relative of Himiko named Iyo, a girl of thirteen, was then made queen and order was restored."

Japanese sources make no mention of Himiko, but some scholars have sought to link her with other powerful queens of around this time.

JINGŪ & THE SEVEN-BRANCHED SWORD

Empress Jingū is said to have reigned from 201-269 CE following the death of her husband, Emperor Chūai. Chūai died without any obvious heir, and Jingū acted as regent for their unborn child. The Nihon Shoki gives an account of her rule and the many acts of warfare she carried out.

THE TŌDAIJIYAMA SWORD

The Kofun tombs of Japan were the burial sites of important Japanese people – people who were often sent to the afterlife with rich grave goods like swords

In the 140-metre-long tomb at Tōdaijiyama, one sword was found that revealed much about Japan in the 2nd century CE.

Inside the tomb were 29 iron swords. One of these, 1.1 metres long, was inlaid with a Chinese inscription in gold, reading: "This ornate sword was manufactured in an auspicious day of the fifth month in the... Zhongping era. The metal from which it has been wrought has been refined many times; it is pure... The fortune of the one who wears it will accord with the stars..." The Zhongping era refers to the rule of the Chinese Emperor Ling of Han, which spanned from 184 to 189 CE.

Was this sword sent from China to a Japanese king? All we can know is that the sword was a treasured item. The tomb it was found in was built in the 4th century, 200 years after the sword was first forged. Other inscribed swords are known, but the Tōdaijiyama Sword is by far the earliest.

ABOVE Kofun tombs were large mounds built for important people and often included rich burial goods like the Tōdaijiyama Sword

ABOVE Jōmon culture flourished in Japan for 10,000 years and its extraordinary pottery productions give tantalising clues into their society

As soon as Jingū came to the throne, she sought to put down potential rebellions. We are told that one village leader, Hashiro Kumawashi, would not obey imperial decrees because he was "a fellow of powerful frame, and had wings on his body, so that he could fly, and with them soar aloft". Jingū struck down the rebel and pacified the region. In one area she avoided battle by executing the sister of an obstreperous general as a warning.

Jingū's greatest exploit, however, was her invasion of Korea. She announced that she "intended in person to chastise the West". Understanding that it was a patriarchal society that she was attempting to lead, she informed her army: "Although I am a woman, and a feeble woman too, I will for a while borrow the outward appearance of a man, and force myself to adopt manly counsels."

With a mighty fleet and army, Jingū crossed the sea, taking up a battle-axe herself. When the enemy king saw the forces arrayed against him, he surrendered, completely and utterly. Other kings and lords also offered rich annual tributes to Jingū. After returning to Japan, she finally gave birth to her husband's heir - a full three years after his death. Much, it may be assumed, is legendary in the tales of Jingū, but many historians do believe that there was a reigning empress around this time to whom myths and tales of Jingū were later attached.

In the Japanese account of her life, we are told that a "seven-branched" sword was presented to Empress Jingū as part of the tribute. Intriguingly, a sword with seven branches off the main blade still exists today. Held in the Isonokami Shrine in Nara prefecture, its Chinese inscription says: "Never before has there been such a blade. The crown prince of the king of Baekje, who lives under august sounds, had this sword made for King of Wa in the hope that it might be passed on to later generations." Baekje was a kingdom in Korea and this sword, along with the legend of Jingū, may tell us much about the relationship between Japan and Korea in antiquity.

UNIFICATION IN THE KOFUN PERIOD

Empress Jingū is generally considered the last ruler of the Yayoi period. The Kofun period that followed is marked by the growing power of the Yamato emperors, descendants of Jingū. Their increasing power is seen in the large Kofun tombs that they were buried in, from which the period takes its name.

These graves are packed with sophisticated arms and armour. Swords have been found with glittering, gilded hilts shaped like animals from myth. Iron armour is often decorated with bronze and gold. These implements of war became necessary as the Yamato sought to increase their power and territory.

At the court in Yamato, the emperors - or Ōkimi, meaning great king, as they called themselves - ruled over a complex web of clans. Some clans were given special roles; the Otomo and Mononobe were often placed in charge of the military, while others served ritual roles or as ministers of state. Inconvenient sons who might otherwise have muddied the line of the imperial succession were sometimes given new surnames and roles, occasionally creating new clans in the process.

Thanks to clay models left as grave offerings from this period, we know that there was a highly developed cavalry that rode horses with saddles and stirrups. These Haniwa figures also show soldiers in suits of armour made from overlapping plates and armed with a sword worn at the hip. Using clan leaders to muster and command armies, the Yamato emperors were able to subjugate the southern half of Japan under their rule.

Japan continued to receive migrants from East Asia throughout the Kofun period. As well as introducing the Chinese writing system and methods of organising an imperial court, many immigrants rose to prominent positions. The incoming people were called Toraijin, and by the 9th century, nearly one-quarter of the clans in the Honshu region could trace their ancestry back to ancestors from outside Japan.

THE GRASS-CUTTING SWORD

Each person who takes the Chrysanthemum Throne of Japan is presented with three legendary items

Japan's imperial regalia consists of an ancient gem, a sacred mirror, and a sword known as Kusanagi-no-Tsurugi - the Grass-Cutting Sword.

According to a legend set down in Kojiki, a 7th-century chronicle, this famous sword was discovered in a battle between a god and a monstrous eight-headed serpent. Once the beast was slain, Kusanagi-no-Tsurugi was found inside its tail. The sword then passed to the goddess Amaterasu, from whom all Japanese emperors are said to be descended.

The sword was once used to protect the emperor when fire spread across a field. The warrior holding it hacked down the burning grass to put out the fire and discovered with each stroke that he could control the direction of the wind.

According to one record, the original sword was lost in the Battle of Dan-no-ura when it was thrown into the sea to prevent it being captured. The sword currently used at coronations may therefore be an ancient replica. The regalia are closely guarded today so it seems unlikely whether scientific analysis will ever be done to determine the truth of the matter.

ABOVE The legendary Grass-Cutting Sword earned its name when Prince Yamato Takeru used it to slash down burning grass to save his emperor

RIGHT Empress Jingū received divine aid in her conquest of Korea and extracted yearly tribute from the kings she conquered

The migrants also brought with them Buddhism for the first time, marking the start of the Asuka Period. In Japanese tradition, Buddhism came to Japan when a king from Korea sent Emperor Kinmei Buddhist images and texts in 552 CE. The emperor is said to have declared: "Never have I heard of such an exquisite teaching." But while he may have been impressed, several clans were not so taken with Buddhism. The Mononobe and Nakatomi clung to the traditional teachings of Shinto, believing that Buddhism would harm the relationship with the kami spirits and thus Japan. While Buddhism was not made the official religion, the Soga clan was allowed to adopt it.

The Soga clan was influential at court and several of its members married into the imperial family. Kinmei's son, Emperor Bidatsu, married a daughter of the Soga clan as his second wife. When Bidatsu died, conflict broke out, with the Soga looking to place the emperor's younger, Soga, son on the throne.

At the Battle of Mount Shigi, the Soga triumphed. According to some, this was through divine aid when they invoked Buddhist symbols. What is known is that an arrow struck down the head of the Mononobe clan, his closest advisers were killed, and his troops scattered. The Soga now firmly embedded Buddhism into Japanese culture.

They continued to influence imperial politics until 645 when the leader of the Nakatomi clan conspired with Prince Ōe to assassinate a member of the Soga clan. This was done in front of the reigning Empress Kōgyoku. Shocked by the murder, she abdicated in favour of her brother. The Asuka period came to an end with the Taika Reforms brought in by Prince Ōe that saw greater centralisation of power in the hands of the emperor. Clans were still influential, but much of their ability to control the throne was removed, limiting their overall power in the imperial court and making it a little harder for one clan to influence the ruler

EMPRESS KŌKEN & THE MONK DŌKYŌ

In 749 CE, an imperial princess took the throne as Empress Kōken. Her father had no direct male heir and ruled alongside her. When he died in 756, his will stated that Kōken's heir would be Prince Funado. However, Kōken was convinced by the powerful Fujiwara no Nakamaro that Funado was insufficiently loyal to the throne and that he should be replaced by Prince Oi. As soon as this was done, conspiracies sprang up not only to return Funado to the line of succession, but to remove Empress Kōken from power.

The conspiracy was soon uncovered and Kōken issued orders to her guards to arrest all involved. The Japanese history Shoku Nihongi goes into great detail about how the conspirators were captured, tortured and forced to confess. Empress Kōken issued an edict that told her subjects how the conspirators planned to kill Nakamaro, steal the seals and ritual objects of the crown, and replace her on the throne.

After the attempted coup, Nakamaro became more powerful. Vast revenues were entrusted to him as well as control of the military. In 757, Kōken abdicated the throne, apparently willingly, to Prince Oi, who became Emperor Junnin. Nakamaro remained one of the leading statesmen at court despite the change in monarch.

Kōken continued to be a power at court, but she fell ill in 761. The cure was found through Dōkyō, a Buddhist monk and son of a minor clan. Soon he was attending court with the former empress and some believed that the two had become lovers.

When Kōken recovered, she returned to court, but, in 762, she declared that the Emperor Junnin was not acting as a ruler should. She issued an edict that would make Junnin a mere figurehead while all real power resided with her. Threatened by the return of Kōken and an increasingly powerful Dōkyō, Nakamaro raised a rebellion.

Nakamaro attempted to seize the insignia and seals of government as well as replacing the compliant Junnin with a stronger emperor. Forced to flee the capital, Nakamaro led his forces east, but imperial troops sent by Kōken blocked his path. When battle turned against Nakamaro he tried to escape on a boat across Lake Biwa. He was captured and, alongside his family, executed. His head was taken to decorate the palace walls.

Empress Kōken now deposed Junnin entirely and retook the throne for herself under the title Empress Shōtoku, with the loyal Dōkyō by

"BY THE 9TH CENTURY, NEARLY ONE-QUARTER OF THE CLANS IN THE HONSHU REGION COULD TRACE THEIR ANCESTRY BACK TO ANCESTORS FROM OUTSIDE JAPAN"

her side. Unfortunately, there was no end to the power and wealth Dōkyō desired. In 768 a message was sent from the Uza Shrine saying that the gods wanted Dōkyō to be emperor. Shōtoku was puzzled by this divine order so she sent a messenger to confirm that this was really what the gods desired. The oracle replied:

"Since the establishment of our state, the distinction between lord and subject has been fixed. Never has there been an occasion when a subject was made lord. The throne of the Heavenly Sun Succession shall be given to one of the imperial lineage; wicked persons should immediately be swept away."

Dōkyō was seen as a grasping usurper and his hold on power began to loosen. When Empress Shōtoku died in 770, he was removed from every office he held and forced into exile in a low-ranking monastery.

THE FUJIWARA CLAN

Nakamaro was just one member of the powerful Fujiwara clan. His defeat did not lead to their destruction. Many of the clan had been opposed to his high-handed ways and refused to be drawn into his rebellion. They remained at court even when Dōkyō was in the ascendancy.

With the death of Kōken and the banishment of Dōkyō, the clan waxed ever more powerful. They came to marry into the imperial family, served as regents and governors, and chose emperors as they willed. The rise of the samurai and professional soldiers grew under the Fujiwara as Japan moved into the Heian period.

THE CONQUEST OF NORTHERN HONSHU

NORTHERN HONSHU WAS NOT ALWAYS PART OF JAPAN; ITS COLONISATION AND CONQUEST, AND THE DYNAMIC RESPONSE BY THE EMISHI EVEN AFTER THEIR MILITARY DEFEAT, HAD A FAR-REACHING INFLUENCE ON JAPANESE POLITICAL AND MILITARY HISTORY

Before its annexation by the Yamato court, northern Honshu was called Michinoku: "beyond where the road ends". In the 7th century, the court's meaningful sphere of control extended as far as Shirakawa Barrier (Shirakawa no seki), a government outpost in modern-day Fukushima prefecture, for a very long time.

Shirakawa Barrier was so far from central Japan that even in later poetry, "Shirakawa Barrier" survived as a euphemism evoking distance. Beyond Shirakawa Barrier in the mountains to the north and east lived the people whom the Yamato state collectively called Emishi - barbarians. They were people who stubbornly refused to submit to the Yamato aegis.

There's some debate as to whether or not the Emishi had a state or states like the Yamato court, but from the Yamato perspective, theirs was foreign land regardless. The colonisation and conquest of northern Honshu, and the dynamic response to that conquest by the Emishi even after their military defeat, had a far-reaching influence on Japanese political and military history.

In the face of this military threat at and beyond its northern borders, the Yamato state steadily expanded its regional control through force. Colonisation, open combat, and a line of fortress-settlements pushed them north over the years. Yamato soldiers were posted to the region as colonists, and as a deterrent against Emishi uprising. As Suzuki Takuya notes in the book *Emishi to Tōhoku Sensō*, from 701 through the late 9th century, the number of Yamato troops rose from 6,000 to 10,000 in the year 768, before settling at around 8,000.

LEFT Great Wisdom Sutra from the Chusonji Temple Sutra Collection

Together with this buildup, in the 8th century Yamato state also established gold mines in Mutsu. The colonisation of Emishi land was thus lucrative.

By the late 8th century, the Yamato court's northern holdings were governed from Fort Taga (Tagajō), a government outpost and military installation just east of modern-day Sendai. Like other provincial capitals in the empire, Fort Taga was the seat of a civil administration. But because this was the edge of empire, it was also the headquarters for a special peacekeeping officer, the Commanding General for Pacification. Together with this, the court divided this newly annexed land into two provinces, Mutsu and Dewa, which endured in some form until the launch of the modern prefecture system in the 1870s.

But Emishi resistance to this foreign authority continued despite the presence of troops. Emishi murdered a Yamato official in 720, and launched a rebellion. The court soon dispatched a punitive expedition in response, and issued an edict ordering land cultivation, which would further bring the land in line with Yamato norms, making it easier to control.

After further revolts in Mutsu in 774, and in Dewa in 777, Emishi rebels burned Fort Taga in 780 and killed local government officials in a revolt led by one-time Yamato ally Korehari no Azamaro. Azamaro had previously led Yamato-allied Emishi troops in support of action against unsubjugated Emishi in Mutsu. Michishima Ōtate, a local Yamato-born resident, apparently taunted Azamaro for his foreign ancestry, which reportedly provoked the revolt. Azamaro's men quickly murdered both Michishima and Ki no Hirozumi, a court noble also antagonistic to Azamaro who was posted to the region. This rebellion raged for over half a year.

ABOVE A hall at Mōtsū-ji, one of the Northern Fujiwara family temples in Hiraizumi

RIGHT Date Masamune's letter to Pope Paul V in 1613, where he refers to himself as "King of Oshu in the Empire of Japan"

Things only worsened for the Yamato court, culminating in the particularly large, late-8th- century Emishi rebellion led by Aterui, who lived in Isawa, one of the Inner Six Counties in what's now Iwate prefecture, where he commanded a significant following. The revolt lasted for several years, until Aterui's defeat and execution in 802.

"THE FUSHŪ KEPT UP A CONTINUITY WITH THEIR NON-YAMATO ROOTS, HOLDING ONTO THEIR LANDS"

That year, a Yamato army under Sakanoue no Tamuramaro crushed further concerted Emishi resistance. Tamuramaro is one of the first people in Japan to have received the title "barbarian-subduing generalissimo"- sei-i taishogun - at a time when this title was given to the commanders of major expeditionary forces dispatched against foreign enemies. He secured Aterui's surrender and reasserted the court's authority in the Tōhoku region.

Tamuramaro's forces further expanded political and military control by building new fortifications. They also moved the regional government's seat from Fort Taga to Fort Isawa, in what is now southern Iwate. Locally based Yamato forces soon built other, more northerly forts. Yet this didn't end the uprisings: another in 878 saw Yamato outposts in Dewa destroyed. Again, it was some time before Yamato forces were able to respond and reassert their control.

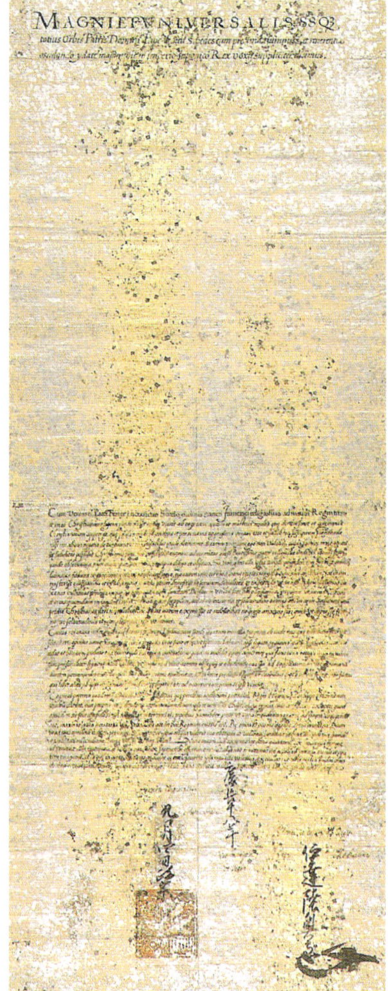

As the Yamato government, newly ensconced in Heian-kyō (modern Kyoto), strengthened and solidified its control over the north, it divided the Emishi into two groups: fushū and emishi. The fushū were the "surrendered barbarians" or "captives", Emishi who submitted to the court's authority and assimilated at least some of Yamato culture. But as historian Mimi Hall Yiengpruksawan notes, the fushū kept up a continuity with their non-Yamato roots, holding onto their lands, gods, and even their weapons for the next several centuries. They were the court's regional allies, called upon to join military campaigns and contribute government levies and projects. Leaders of major fushū families could also hold the title of "fushū chief" (fushūchō), which recognised their preeminence but also brought them at least nominally into the Yamato government's political orbit. Meanwhile, the court continued to label Emishi those northerners who did not submit, and who remained outside the court's control and the Yamato cultural sphere.

A fushū family that rose to prominence in the Heian era was the Northern Fujiwara, whose first stronghold was Tamuramaro's old Fort Isawa. This was a family of mixed Yamato-Emishi origin, which ruled from its second stronghold, Hiraizumi, for four generations.

Although it was kin to the princely Fujiwara family that frequently held political power at the Kyoto court, the Northern Fujiwara family made no secret of its Emishi heritage. Northern Fujiwara founder Fujiwara no Kiyohira (1056-1128) and his grandson Hidehira (1122-87) understood that their land lay "inside" and "outside" the empire, and took advantage of that position, maintaining connections with Kyoto while each called himself "chief of the barbarians".

The view from Kyoto held that the Northern Fujiwara were cultured, but also part barbarian. All Fujiwara lords starting with Kiyohira held some sort of court rank or office, but some in Kyoto felt that this

NORTHERN HONSHU AFTER THE EMISHI

The story of northern Honshu as a semi-autonomous region not quite adhering to the rules of the rest of Japan continued well past Minamoto no Yoritomo's conquest of the Northern Fujiwara lands. Yoritomo stationed the Isawa family at Fort Taga, appointing it to the office of Mutsu Caretaker (Ōshū Rusushoku), with considerable local autonomy.

The posting of local representatives with semi-autonomous authority continued under the succeeding Ashikaga shogunate (1336-1573), with the posting of tandai, or commissioners. Finally, in the Warring States era, the House of Date made itself into the region's political centre of gravity, during the rule of its most renowned daimyo, Date Masamune (1567-1636). Masamune was like the Northern Fujiwara a patron of the arts and religion, and it's thanks to his and his descendants' efforts that many of the temples and other historic locations of the Northern Fujiwara survive to the present.

In his correspondence with European heads of state, Masamune called himself "King of Ōshū in the Empire of Japan"- that is, King of Mutsu, the former Michinoku. And two centuries later, his descendants led the domains of northern Honshu in the Northern Alliance, which fought to defend northern Honshu's autonomy during the Boshin War. One can't help but think that the Northern Fujiwara would be proud.

was improper because of their Emishi heritage. Others feared the Northern Fujiwara were secretly commanders of a barbarian horde that could spill over into the rest of Japan without warning. This fear was part of what precipitated the northern military campaigns of Minamoto no Yoritomo, the first Kamakura shogun.

Regardless of their reputation in Kyoto as quasi-barbarians, the Fujiwara were wealthy thanks in part to the gold that the Yamato court had once discovered in the region, and were thus not only in a position to field fighting forces but also to be patrons of the arts and the centre of a Buddhist cultural sphere.

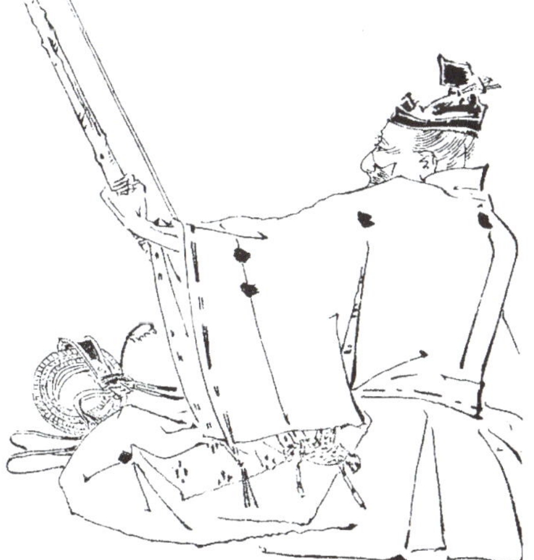

ABOVE Northern Fujiwara ruler Fujiwara no Hidehira, as depicted by Kikuchi Yōsai

Theirs was a syncretic Buddhism, one that incorporated Heian-era Shinto deities as well as old Emishi deities that were still worshipped in northern Honshu. Kyoto developed its own Buddhist culture, but Hiraizumi's was different because it merged those Emishi spiritual traditions with Buddhism.

Chūson-ji and Mōtsū-ji, two of the Northern Fujiwara family's major temples, were named a UNESCO World Heritage site in 2011. The temples were where pathbreaking haiku poet Matsuo Bashō visited in the 17th century and wrote his famous poem about summer grass as the last remnant of warriors' dreams.

Protected by politics, soldiering and force of the dharma, the Northern Fujiwara state and society flourished until its sudden, violent destruction in 1189, before the still greater armed might of the armies Minamoto no Yoritomo raised from the Kantō region. But northern Honshu, now known as the Tōhoku ('East-North') region, remained a politically semi-autonomous region into the late Edo period. While it is no longer the northernmost part of Japan, it does remain a significantly rural region today.

And what of the title of sei-i taishōgun once held by Tamuramaro in his campaigns against the Emishi? This title went on to far greater fame as the honorific that would be held by three successive dynasties from the 12th to the 19th century. We remember it today in its abbreviated form: shogun.

ABOVE Cenotaph to Emishi leaders Aterui and more in modern Hirakata, Osaka prefecture

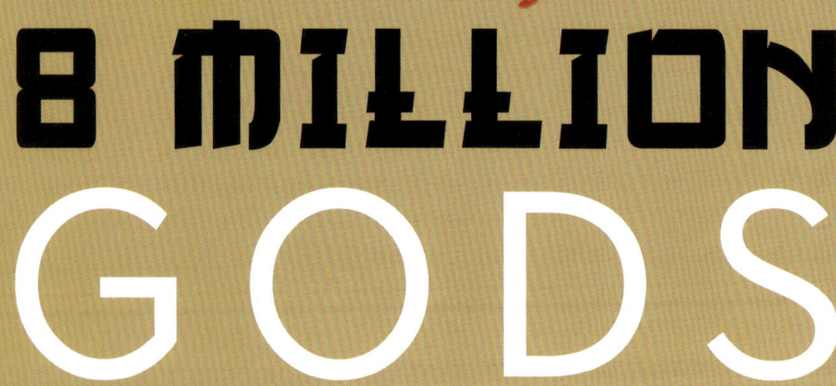

8 MILLION GODS

WHAT ARE THESE BEINGS CALLED KAMI, WHAT DO THEY REPRESENT, AND WHAT DO THEY MEAN TO THE PEOPLE OF JAPAN?

Despite the majority of Japanese citizens today describing themselves as non-religious, Shintoism is prevalent in the country and its culture. Yet, Shinto is not your typical religion. It does not follow any ancient text or act in accordance with any doctrines, but it instead offers ways for people to show their appreciation for various aspects of life and the world we inhabit.

The word Shinto means "The Way of the Gods", and these beings or gods are known as kami. There is no concrete definition of kami and so they are not easy to characterise. These gods can represent specific locations, animals and objects or embody them in general. For example, a river may be home to a specific kami, but at the same time it also houses the kami of rivers generally. Which kami is more important is irrelevant - what matters most is people recognising the existence of kami.

There are thousands of Shinto shrines across Japan and these can be identified by the big, red gates known as 'torii' at their entrances. These shrines house kami and people can enter them to show thanks to kami or pray for good fortune.

Many of the myths around kami and their origins come from the *Kojiki*, one of Japan's oldest surviving texts that was written around 712 CE. The *Kojiki* is split into three books, with the first explaining the creation of the world by the gods of heaven and how the imperial family came to rule Japan. These gods of heaven are known as amatsukami; who birthed Izanagi and Izanami, two siblings that created our world. These two kami would have three offspring, Amaterasu, Tsukuyomi and Susanoo, who are known as the 'three noble children'. Amaterasu, the sun goddess, is said to be the ancestor of Japan's imperial family and one of the rulers of the heavenly realm. It is also believed that the emperors of Japan are descended from kami and that they become one after death. Tsukuyomi is the moon goddess who rules the night, while Susanoo is the storm god who represents violent natural forces and controls the oceans.

As for the other kami, there are three types: Amatsukami, gods of Heaven; Kunitsukami, gods of the earth; and ya-o-yorozu no kami, the countless millions of other gods that inhabit or embody aspects of various objects and places. The people of Japan show their respect to these kami by offering food or drink and holding festivals in their honour, while showing them disrespect can invite bad fortune.

MAIN The sun goddess Amaterasu is one of Shinto's major kami along with Tsukuyomi and Susanoo. These are known as the 'three noble children'

RIGHT There can be kami for things such as rivers, mountains and trees in general, as well as kami for individual rivers, mountains and trees

FAR RIGHT The *Kojiki* is one of Japan's oldest texts. Written in 712, it describes different kami as well as the creation of the universe

KAMI

BECOMING JAPAN THE ASUKA PERIOD

THE RISE OF IMPERIAL POWER AND A FLOURISHING OF THE ARTS AND CULTURE IN JAPAN CAN BE TRACED TO THE EVENTS OF THE ASUKA PERIOD

The Asuka period (592 to 710 CE) was a pivotal one in the development of the culture of Japan and is regarded as the beginning of Japan's Classical Age. Japan's modern name, Nippon, was first adopted in this time and shows an increasing awareness of the potential of Japan. Nippon, which means "the sun's origin" and is widely translated as "the land of the rising sun", set itself apart from the lands to the west where the sun set.

ABOVE Empress Suiko was the first ruling Empress of Japan and her reign marked the beginning of the reforms in the Asuka period

MOVING POLITICS

The Asuka period takes its name from the move of the imperial capital to the Asuka region in Yamato Province. Each time the Emperor died a new palace was constructed and the capital moved but during this period most remained in the Asuka region. We know much about Asuka period politics because this was the first period of Japanese history where actual historical events can be distinguished from legendary and folkloric narratives.

The government of Japan at this time was controlled by the powerful heads of the great clans. These families played vital roles in the administration of the state. The Emperor was notable for his role in the rituals thought necessary for the maintenance of divine favour. Before the Asuka period the Mononobe and Soga clans had contended for supremacy. The Mononobe were conservative and inward-looking while the Soga were more open to allowing foreign influences, such as Buddhism. At the Battle of Mount Shigi in 587 CE the Mononobe forces were defeated by the Soga, their leaders killed, and the Soga became the most powerful clan in Japan. Marriage to the imperial family led to generations of emperors having Soga blood.

With the backing of the Soga, the emperor began to have more influence in the control of government, if only with the assent of the Soga leaders. In 593 CE the Empress Suiko, the first of Japan's eight female rulers, came to the throne after the previous Emperor Sushun was assassinated on the orders of one of the Soga. She appointed her nephew Prince Shōtoku as her regent. Many of the reforms of this period are credited to Shōtoku.

POWERFUL REGENTS

In the defeat of the Mononobe clan, Shōtoku is said to have called on the Buddha to aid the Soga forces. As a devoted Buddhist, Shōtoku founded the first Buddhist temple in Japan, Shitennō-ji, employing Korean builders. Yet Shōtoku also continued to visit Shinto shrines and a distinctive Japanese syncretism between the two faiths would continue to develop. According to legend, a sweet smelling wood drifted over the sea to Japan in this time and when burned produced aromatic smoke, and incense became central to Japanese rituals.

LEFT The Asuka period saw a growth in literacy with poetry composed by the elite members of society as in this illustrated poem by Emperor Tenji

It was Shōtoku who first referred to Japan as the land of the rising sun. When the Emperor of Sui in China wrote to the Empress he said "the sovereign of Sui respectfully inquires about the sovereign of Wa". Shōtoku responded with a letter addressed "From the sovereign of the land of the rising sun to the sovereign of the land of the setting sun". This is said to have angered the Emperor of China as it suggested that the Japanese leader was of the same rank as himself.

Under Empress Suiko the business of the government was reformed to be more like the Chinese model. Confucian doctrines from China insisted on service and deference to those in power. The centrality of the Emperor in Chinese government and society was an attractive one for Japanese rulers to follow as they struggled with their own powerful nobility.

Other reforms weakened the grip select families had on the levers of government. While positions had been decided on heredity, a new system known as The Twelve Level Cap and Rank System was adopted in 603 CE. This assigned ranks and powers, denoted by different coloured silk caps, to officials. Those who were skilled could rise through the ranks in a more meritocratic way allowing for some amount of social mobility, though still tightly controlled. The Seventeen-Article Constitution promulgated by Shōtoku in 604 CE is regarded as one of the world's first written constitutions but deals mainly with the behaviour of government officials.

CONTROLLING THE SOGA

Empress Kōgyoku came to the throne in 642 CE but the influence of the Soga clan was challenged almost immediately. Many were upset by the patronage that the Soga gave to Buddhism and the control they had of key Buddhist sites.

"BUDDHISM TOOK ON THE ROLE OF A STATE RELIGION"

A plot was hatched by the minister Fujiwara no Kamatari and Prince Nakano Ōe to purge the Soga. In 645 CE, during a court ceremony, they struck in an event known as the Isshi Incident. The palace gates were locked and a spear hidden in the hall where the Empress was in attendance. Soga no Iruka was attacked in front of the Empress but begged for mercy. As the Empress retired to consider the matter, guardsmen slaughtered him. His father committed suicide and the Soga clan was left leaderless. Empress Kōgyoku abdicated the throne in favour of a male relative, though she would later retake the throne as a regent.

Following the fall of the Soga the Buddhist sites and hierarchy were taken under direct Imperial control. The Emperor appointed ten chief priests who were told to instruct all Buddhists on the loyalty they owed to the Emperor above all others. Three secular officials were also appointed to ensure Buddhist worship and practice conformed to the needs of the Imperial court. Under these reforms Buddhism took on the role of a state religion which existed to serve the needs of the crown. By adopting Buddhism the elite may have hoped to raise the status of Japan, which was considered barbarous by many in China and Korea.

Fujiwara no Kamatari and Prince Nakano Ōe retained the real power after the Isshi incident. They launched the Taika Reforms based on Chinese models and philosophies. These all tended to centralise power in the hands of the Imperial Court. Provinces were created under the control of governors who were to survey their land, redistribute it, and tax it accordingly. All free men and women were allotted a small amount of land to farm. By issuing regular salaries to officials the Emperor linked wealth and security to loyalty.

RIGHT The powerful regent Prince Shōtoku was integral to introducing Buddhist worship to Japan through his support of temples, art, and literary works

Weapons were to be taken from private ownership and held by the government. Landholders were placed under obligation to the throne. A bureaucracy was created to limit the independence of powerful local leaders. Not all of these were successful and clans maintained much of their strength.

Systems of Chinese law and administration were introduced based on first hand knowledge of envoys sent from Japan. Householders were expected to draw up documents known as koseki which listed the inhabitants of their home to aid in taxation and the levying of

TIMELINE OF ASUKA HISTORY CE

DEFINING MOMENT

PRINCE SHŌTOKU MADE REGENT

Prince Shōtoku, son of a previous emperor, is appointed as regent for the empress. As a supporter of Buddhism he encourages the erection of temples in Japan. Envoys to China bring back knowledge of their system of government that he implements to increase Imperial power. Prince Shōtoku also writes the first legal codes, histories, and Buddhist texts in Japan and stimulates interest in Chinese literature. It is Prince Shōtoku who first refers to Japan as "the land of the rising sun" in correspondence with the Emperor of China.

592 — 593 — 603 — 608 — 7TH CENTURY

592: SUIKO BECOMES EMPRESS

Empress Suiko ascends the throne after her predecessor is assassinated. The imperial court in Asuka begins to centralise its power. Under her rule reforms to administration and law begin to be enacted.

603: TWELVE LEVEL CAP SYSTEM

The Twelve Level Cap System is introduced at court to define the seniority of officials in Imperial service. Each colour of cap denoted a different rank. Instead of inherited positions the best qualified person is appointed to a role.

608: SENT TO CHINA

Takamuko no Kuromaro is dispatched to China to study their system of government. He remains there for 32 years and when he returns is pivotal in Japanese reforms. He is granted the title "National Scholar".

7TH CENTURY: NEW ARTISTIC STYLES

With the rise of Buddhism new styles of painting, sculpture, and architecture are imported from Asia. Tori Busshi's statues of the Buddha become emblematic of the fusion of Japanese design with Buddhist iconography.

TOP At the Battle of Baekgang a Japanese fleet was destroyed as it came to the aid of an allied kingdom in Korea

ABOVE Though the power of the clans was reduced in the Asuka period violence was provoked when some became too influential, as at the Isshi Incident

troops. Wooden strips with these registers written on them have been discovered from the 7th century.

WAR & LAW

Japanese involvement in south-east Asia was not limited to importing ideas and goods. In 663 CE Prince Ōe sent a fleet and thousands of men to aid Baekje, one of the kingdoms of Korea, against an incursion from Tang China. At the battle of Baekgang the Japanese forces suffered their largest defeat in pre-modern history and lost a key ally with the collapse of Baekje. Perhaps 10,000 Japanese warriors were killed and Japan was left as the sole enemy of Tang China in the region. Efforts were made to strengthen the defences of those parts of Japan close to China in case of an invasion, while envoys were sent to China to reestablish peaceful relations between the two countries. Following the war there was a wave of immigration to Japan from the fallen kingdom which furthered the influence of mainland ideas.

In 668 CE Prince Nakano Ōe ascended the throne as Emperor Tenji, having been crown prince during the preceding reigns. He issued one of the first collections of laws in Japanese history and continued with reforms aimed at drawing more power into the Emperor's hands. In 672 CE Tenji died and left the throne to his son Prince Ōtomo after previously favouring his brother Prince Ōama. Prince Ōama raised a rebellion, known as the Jinshin War, against his nephew and defeated him in battle. After less than a year on the throne Ōtomo killed himself and Ōama came to power as the Emperor Tenmu.

DEFINING MOMENT

THE ISSHI INCIDENT

The Soga clan was one of the most powerful in the state and held many important roles. Jealousy of their power and influence on the throne leads Nakatomi no Kamatari and Prince Naka no Ōe (the future Emperor Tenji) to plot their downfall. At a court function Soga no Iruka is attacked in front of Empress Kōgyoku. As the empress leaves, he is killed. The Soga clan is targeted and removed from power. Empress Kōgyoku abdicates and Prince Naka no Ōe becomes the most powerful lord under the following Emperors.

DEFINING MOMENT

FIRST COINS

In 708 the first written mention of coins minted in Japan is made. These Wadōkaichin are made in emulation of Chinese coins and point towards an increase in trade both domestically and internationally. As the state becomes more powerful and large it becomes cumbersome to transport goods for trade instead of money. Archaeology suggests coins were made before this but with official recognition a complex economic system forms. It becomes possible for the Emperor to issue salaries to officials and hire workers efficiently. Trade and taxation are made simpler.

645 · 646 · 661 · 668 · 672 · 708 · 710

TAIKA REFORMS

Following the Isshi Incident a series of reforms based on Chinese models is announced. These include land reforms, the appointment of governors, taxation, military service, and laws. They bring more authority and power to the Emperor.

FIGHTING IN KOREA

A fleet of Japanese ships and a large army is dispatched to aid the Japanese allies in Korea against Chinese forces. At the Battle of Baekgang in 663 the Japanese forces are completely destroyed.

FIRST LAW CODE

Emperor Tenji orders the codification of all Japanese laws into a single work. This Ōmi Code consists of 22 volumes and is expanded and edited in future law codes issued in the Asuka period.

CIVIL WAR

Following the death of Emperor Tenji a civil war breaks out between his brother and son as to who will succeed. The war is won by his brother who becomes Emperor Tenmu. He increases the power of the Japanese military.

CAPITAL MOVES TO NARA

Empress Gemmei moves with the Imperial court to its new seat, modelled after a Chinese city, in Nara province. The Asuka period ends. The reforms to Japanese governance begun in Asuka continue to shape social evolution.

> "JITŌ HELPED TO CONTINUE THE REFORMATION OF JAPANESE GOVERNMENT ALONG CHINESE LINES"

While historians refer to earlier rulers as emperor or empress it was only under Tenmu that they were given the title Tennō (emperor); before this other titles were generally used. Tenmu's reign was marked by continued efforts to strengthen the position of the Emperor. Perhaps given that a rebellion had raised him to the throne Tenmu sought to reinforce his military position. The administration of the army was reformed and new fortifications were built to protect the lands close to the capital. By placing some of his many sons into important roles in the government he further reduced the power of the clans to control him.

Emperor Tenmu took his role as head of the traditional Shinto worship seriously. He sent his daughter to act as the high priestess of the shrine dedicated to Amaterasu - from whom the Imperial family claimed descent. Yet he also continued to patronise Buddhism. He encouraged homeowners to have both a Shinto altar and a statue of the Buddha. He also forbade the eating of domesticated animals during a certain part of the year, though those lords who had ample hunting grounds could still eat deer and other wild game. The structures of Buddhism came under increasing control of the Imperial throne as only those given permission could become Buddhist monks or priests.

EMPRESSES IN CHARGE

Following Tenmu's death in 686 CE his wife, and niece, took the throne as Empress Jitō. Jitō helped to continue the reformation of Japanese government along Chinese lines by insisting that her officials study the laws of Tang China. She ruled directly for eleven years before abdicating in favour of her grandson. She relinquished the crown but remained a powerful influence at court. After abdication she was given the title of Daijō Tennō. For much of Japanese history emperors would follow this path by retiring but remaining potent forces in the government when they became Daijō Tennō.

Empress Jitō was succeeded by her grandson Emperor Monmu in 697 CE but when he died young in 707 CE his mother became Empress Genmei. Monmu had planned to transplant the Imperial court to Nara but the preparations for this were not complete by the time he died and it was Genmei who oversaw the move from Asuka in 710 CE. Though she ruled for several more years this is generally considered to be the end of the Asuka period and the culture that flourished there.

Following the move to Nara a poet described the feeling of change for Japan;

"Asuka breezes, which used to flutter the sleeves, of lovely ladies, aimlessly blow on in vain, now that the court moved away."

ASUKA ENLIGHTENMENT

The earliest written documents from Japan date from the Asuka period. They were composed in classical Chinese and use the Chinese writing system. The first Japanese literary works to come be passed down are said to have been written by Prince Shōtoku. They include a commentary on Buddhist texts, which is now considered a national treasure. Shōtoku also wrote two works of history which have not survived.

Literacy in Japan can be traced to China and there was a large influx of texts from China in the Asuka period which influenced much of Japanese literature. Though it was likely only officials and members of the upper classes who could read and write, many masterpieces of literature were produced. In the Man'yōshū, The Collection of Ten Thousand Leaves, 4500 poems are collected which can be dated to the Asuka period. They are written in Classical Japanese as waka, poems in various metres, and which take their name from the old name for Japan, Wa.

This was a period of artistic evolution. Knowledge of the arts could aid a person's rise through society. Yamanoue Okura, a poet of the 7th century, became a minor noble and bureaucrat. Through his works we can understand the feelings of people in Japan at this time. We know that population boomed but also suffered enormous losses due to waves of disease. Okura described losing one of his sons, who he likened to a white pearl, to illness. After the child wasted away we are told:

"I stood, I jumped, I stamped,
I shrieked, I lay on the ground,
I beat my breast and wailed.
Yet the child I held so tight
Has flown beyond my clasp.
Is this the way of the world?"

The art of the Asuka period showed the transformations which were occurring in Japan at this time. The introduction of Buddhism created a need for statues to decorate temples. Tori Busshi is considered to be the greatest sculptor of his day. His grandfather immigrated to Japan from the Asian mainland and became a saddle-maker. Tori followed this path and learned many of the skills needed for his later craft.

LEFT Horyu-Ji temple, founded by Prince Shotoku, is one of the oldest wooden buildings in Japan and exemplifies the architectural style of the Asuka period

ABOVE The Asuka Daibutsu is a large bronze statue of Buddha created in 608 CE by the sculptor Tori Busshi for the temple built in Asuka

Tori Busshi was employed by members of the Soga clan and Prince Shōtoku and became one of the most renowned makers of Buddhist imagery. He was highly influenced by the Chinese style of Buddhist rock carvings, but replicated them in gilt bronze. Many works of the Asuka period are ascribed to Tori Busshi or those in his workshop.

As well as works in bronze many sculptures were created from wood. Most of these have not survived but one that does is found in the only surviving Asuka period building. Horyuji Temple contains the oldest wooden buildings in Japan and it also houses a carved Buddha made from camphor wood. The Kudara Kannon stands over 2m tall and was the first item to be designated a national treasure.

The development of Japanese society into more centralised society let to increasingly complex trade and economic relationships. Coins from China dating to the early centuries of the 1st millennium have been archaeologically discovered across Japan. The first coins minted in Japan were made in the Asuka period. In imitation of Chinese coins they are circular with a square hole in the middle. When exactly they were first made is not known. That fact that coins were required points to the development of a society where trading in commodities was no longer possible or desirable in the Asuka period.

BLENDING SHINTO & BUDDHISM

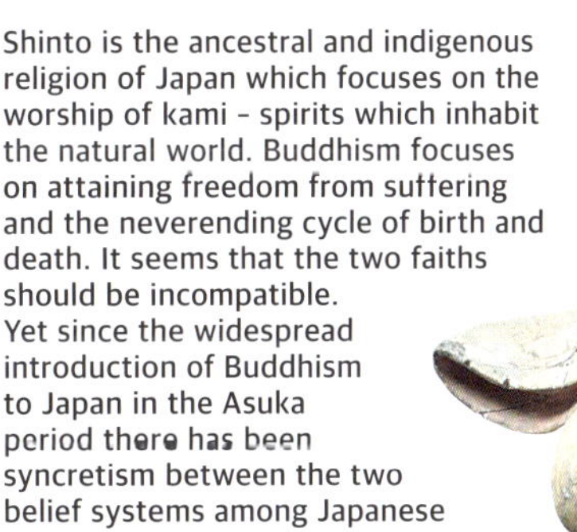

Shinto is the ancestral and indigenous religion of Japan which focuses on the worship of kami - spirits which inhabit the natural world. Buddhism focuses on attaining freedom from suffering and the neverending cycle of birth and death. It seems that the two faiths should be incompatible. Yet since the widespread introduction of Buddhism to Japan in the Asuka period there has been syncretism between the two belief systems among Japanese worshippers.

The joining of Shinto and Buddhism is known as Shinbutsu-shūgō. From the earliest days Buddhist temples were constructed near to Shinto shrines, though the priesthood of the faiths remained separate. The Buddhism which reached Japan had already been changed from the original Buddhism of India by the influence of Chinese culture. This made it more amenable to assimilation into Japanese culture.

Buddhist priests were willing to accept the existence of kami as spirits in need of their care just like all sentient beings. The two religions never completely united but in the minds of most Japanese people they were entirely compatible. For the emperor, both faiths were equally useful as they supported the rightness of their rule.

Today many Japanese are welcomed into the world with Shinto rituals but buried in Buddhist ceremonies. This has led to the saying "Born Shinto, Die Buddhist."

ABOVE Hachiman, a Shinto kami of archery and war, has been incorporated into Buddhist belief as a revered figure on his way to enlightenment

FIVE PROVINCES & SEVEN CIRCUITS

BY THE ASUKA PERIOD MORE OF JAPAN HAD COME UNDER THE SWAY OF THE IMPERIAL THRONE, AND SYSTEMS HAD TO BE CREATED TO ADMINISTER IT

The nation of Japan as it exists today is a long archipelago of islands, yet the Emperor of what would become Japan did not at first rule all of them. The expansion of Japan occurred in stages by military conquest and careful use of influence and patronage. By the Asuka period most of the south of the main island was in the, occasionally nominal, control of the Imperial court. To run the nation efficiently an administrative system had to be created.

The Gokishichidō system, meaning "five provinces and seven circuits", broke the land into units that were controlled by officials appointed by the Imperial court. The five Kinai provinces were those that were in and around the capitals at Nara and Kyoto. They were Yamato, Yamashiro, Kawachi, Settsu, and Izumi.

The seven dō, or circuits, were larger areas radiating away from the central provinces in different directions. They were Tōkaidō (the eastern sea circuit), Tōsandō (the eastern mountain circuit), Hokurikudō (the northern land circuit), San'indō (the 'dark' mountain circuit), San'yōdō (the 'light' mountain circuit), Nankaidō (the southern sea circuit), and Saikaidō (the western seas circuit). Each was itself composed of smaller provinces and all were connected by roads that tied the circuit to the capital. These roads shared the same name as the circuits they ran through.

This system of regional administration was drawn from the Confucian models employed in China at this time which stressed the importance of loyalty to the Emperor. All legitimate power was ultimately derived from him and by appointing governors to the regions the Emperor was delegating some of his power for a limited time to those he could trust. A strict hierarchy of ranks and titles ensured that each position was controlled by Imperial mandate.

The regions created by the five province and seven circuit reforms remained in use in Japan for centuries. How they were incorporated into Japan, administered, and morphed into the prefectures of modern Japan is the history of the nation itself.

LEFT The Gokishichidō system split Japan into Imperial-ruled units

A CENTRE OF POWER

THE KINAI PROVINCES OF JAPAN WERE THE LOCATION OF THE IMPERIAL CAPITAL FOR CENTURIES AND FORMED THE HUB OF IMPERIAL ADMINISTRATION

The Asuka period (592-710 CE) began with the move of the capital from elsewhere in the Yamato province to Asuka. With the move to Asuka came attempts to emulate the Chinese system of government and political forms in a series of legal codifications known as the Ritsuryō. Key to these reforms was the creation of the five provinces at the heart of Japan. The Kanai ("Capital region") provinces would be the home of the Imperial court for over a thousand years.

Japan did not grow from a single source but arose out of the interactions, conflicts, and unifications of various alliances. Kings emerged in Yamato province in the 4th century and did prove key in developing a centralised government. These kings were not all-powerful rulers but had a leading voice in alliances between powerful families. We also have hints of other royal families ruling in other places. The history of this period is contested but it seems that the first permanent capitals were established in the Yamato province at this time rather than following the king wherever he travelled. Large royal burial mounts known as kofun began to appear.

FERTILE GROUND

Yamato was an excellent place to found a nation because of the richness of its agricultural land which could larger numbers of troops and craftsmen. Much of the growth in Yamato's power came from uniting clans through diplomacy and intermarriage. By making allegiance with the Yamato royal family favourable to enmity they grew in prestige. Yet military might must have played some role in the foundation of state. Archaeological finds and historical records show the importance of weapons in this period. The seven-branched sword known as shichishitō was given to a Yamato king and was held as a prized relic at the ancient Isonokami Shrine.

In the 5th century power began to shift westwards from Yamato into the central provinces of Kawachi and Izumi. It was also a period of increasing power for the kings. We know this as the kofun tombs constructed for them grew enormously in size, which must have

ABOVE The establishment of the Imperial palace in the central provinces gave Japan an administrative centre which could be defended and expanded

taken thousands of builders years to complete. The Kawachi province remained important to Imperial politics as the base of power for the influential Mononobe clan. The king was hereditary but seems to have had the power to select the heads of the clans under him from among clan members, giving him some control of these potential rivals.

The seat of the Imperial government continued to move with the accession of each emperor but all stayed within the Kinai provinces. The court would be moved for a number of reasons. Some of the moves seem to have been to remove the new ruler from a place associated with their predecessor and to create for themselves an impressive new palace complex. As the palaces of the Asuka period were made of wood little remains of any of them today. Many of these were practical moves to place the emperor or empress in a position where their attention was most required and to secure their safety.

The geography and history of the Kinai provinces often dictated where power congregated. Moving the capital to the site of an important shrine would help to build the association of the Imperial throne with divinity. In 708 CE the empress Genmei moved the capital to Nara. While she claimed that this was driven by divine signs the location of the city, surrounded on three sides by defensive mountains, and with access to rivers that connected to the sea must have had some obvious attractions.

The government of the Kinai provinces in the Gokishichidō system was designed to keep them loyal to the emperor. According to law codes of the 8th century every person who did not hold a title of nobility was a "state person" - they belonged to the state. All land which could be cultivated for rice was "state land." The government assigned a certain amount of land to each person. From the produce of this land a tax had to be paid. Those who lived in the Kinai provinces only had to pay half of what was required in the outlying regions. They were also exempt from certain other taxes. There were downsides in that sometimes workers could be called to labour on Imperial projects.

CONTROLLING THE CAPITAL

To further centralise power, governors were appointed by the emperor to take charge of each province. They resided in the central town of each province and were responsible for raising taxes and manpower. The governors were often drawn from outside of the clan loyalties of the region and owed their position only to the emperor. Under them came clerks and officials of various ranks in a strict hierarchy.

The management of a region was not always an easy task, even in the central Kinai provinces. A poem from the 8th century describes the fate of Tatsumaro, an official in Settsu province, who was given the task of reallocating state land. He had to work day and night on the project in total obedience to the emperor's command. The strain of overwork pushed him to suicide.

In the Heian period which followed the move to Nara the capital was transferred to Kyoto in the Yashimiro province. From this relocation of the Imperial court in 794 CE until it was moved to Tokyo in 1869, Kyoto remained the seat of the Emperors of Japan. Strife and civil disorder would see powerful warlords and other build up bases of power elsewhere in Japan but the Imperial capital no longer moved with the accession of each emperor.

Much of what is considered Japanese culture today developed from the Imperial court and the Kinai provinces.

"WITH THE MOVE TO ASUKA CAME ATTEMPTS TO EMULATE THE CHINESE SYSTEM OF GOVERNMENT"

HISTORY OF KYOTO

The Japanese Imperial capital of Kyoto was constructed in the 8th century to be a replica of the Chinese Imperial capital of the Tang dynasty at Chang'an. It was part of the importation of Chinese-style governance to Japan. The new capital was originally named Heian-kyō - meaning Tranquil Capital. The city would not always enjoy tranquillity.

At the centre of the city was a large, walled palace complex call the Daidairi. Here, the emperor both lived and managed the state bureaucracy with the help of his ministers. Having brought all power into the palace his courtiers became highly influential in government and social trends. The fashions of court were emulated throughout the country. Art and culture flourished with novels, plays, and paintings emerging from the tastes developed in the city of emperors.

While Kyoto remained the base of the Imperial court it was not spared by the struggles for power. In the Ōnin War of the 15th century much of Kyoto was reduced to rubble when competing armies battled within the walls for control of the emperor. Kyoto was slowly rebuilt and most of the spectacular architecture which attracts tourists to the city today was constructed on the ashes of the old city.

ABOVE The Imperial capital remained at Kyoto for over 1,000 years, though real power was often held by those outside the court

CONQUERING A COUNTRY

BEFORE A NATION CAN BE BROUGHT TOGETHER AS A SINGLE ENTITY, CONTROL MUST FIRST BE EXERTED OVER ITS LAND – BY BATTLE OR MORE SUBTLE METHODS

Japan has been inhabited by humans for at least 40,000 years. For most of this time the people lived in hunter-gatherer communities but the Jomon people of the early millennia BCE achieved high levels of sophistication in pottery and culture. In the first millennium BCE the Yayoi people began to arrive in Japan, probably from the Korean peninsula. They brought with them a language and the cultivation of rice. The population of Japan boomed with increased food resources and larger settlements began to form.

Unfortunately there is no contemporary Japanese literature for these early periods. Chinese sources hint at powerful rulers such as Queen Himiko of the Yamatai kingdom in Japan. However there is much debate as to whether she was a real person. It may be that the Yamato kingdom was a continuation of the earlier Yamatai. Archaeological evidence, together with later texts, helps to untangle how Japan conquered the islands of the nation.

LEGENDARY CONQUESTS

The Yamato kings ruled the central provinces from a very early date, yet there were always rivals. Based on the number of temples and large tombs discovered by archaeologists the Kingdom of Kibi to the west seems to have been just as strong as the Yamato kingdom. A tale written down in the Asuka period hundreds of years later says that in the 4th century a son of the Yamato Emperor Korei called Kibitsu-hiko-no-mikoto slew an ogre called Uri who lived in Ki castle. We now know that Ki castle was the capital of the Kibi kingdom and it may be that this legend reflects the conquest of Kibi by the Yamato kingdom.

Other records show lands being brought into the kingdom by warfare. The 8th century *Kojiki*, the oldest written history of Japan, collected many stories that supposedly record how the Yamato kings became the emperors of all of Japan. According to this telling it was during the reign of Emperor Sujin in the 1st century BC that four generals, known as the Shidō shoguns, were appointed. Each was given a cardinal direction (north, south, east, and west) from the capital and told to ensure that the people there were brought into line with the Emperor's will. In this telling it was Sujin who organised his realm into provinces and set governors under him, though even the existence of Sujin is a matter of debate.

To the west of Yamato, Izumo province was absorbed into the Yamato kingdom by trickery. A rogue prince called Yamato Takeru was sent out by his father to conquer Izumo, but with no hopes of success. He slew the rulers of Izumo by dressing up as a serving woman and sneaking into their tent. There he plied them with alcohol until they became so drunk that he was able to stab them with ease. As the tales of Yamato Takeru also include him slaying evil deities, the historical accuracy of this account must be doubted. However Izumo was indeed incorporated into the Yamato kingdom.

Within the province were several important sites in Shinto. As the Yamato kingdom grew these and other regional holy shrines helped to unify the people as each province could contribute something to the prosperity of the nation through shared religious practice.

The historical record becomes more certain in later centuries thanks to archaeology and written texts with fewer references to clearly legendary events. The large keyhole-shaped tombs known as kofun developed in the Yamato kingdom. By tracing and dating their spread across Japan we can follow if not the direct conquest, at least the

> "THE YAMATO KINGS RULED THE CENTRAL PROVINCES"

RIGHT Forging the nation of Japan was not completed in a single campaign but achieved over centuries of both warfare and diplomacy

ABOVE The samurai armour and style of fighting developed out of the wars that brought the north of Honshu island under the control of the capital

spread of Yamato culture into more distant areas. It is likely that control of the outer regions was hegemonic with the Yamato kings ruling through a complex network of alliances and intermarriage with the most important clans. Provinces presented tribute to the Yamato kings as a sign of their subservience. The possibly legendary Emperor Keitai of the early 6th century was only a distant descendent of a former emperor and seems to have come from Koshi province to the north. In one tale, the people of Koshi later in the 6th century presented the empress with a white deer as tribute.

SUBDUING THE EMISHI

The north of the largest island in Japan was populated by a group of people known as the Emishi that the Yamato regarded as barbarians. Their term for the nebulous frontier between their own lands of those and the Emishi can be translated as "the end of the land". The court in Yamato had only a vague understanding of who the Emishi were, or at least scorned their way of life. "We hear that the Eastern savages are of a violent disposition, and are much given to oppression: their hamlets have no chiefs, their villages no leaders, each is greedy of territory, and they plunder one another." The evidence from archaeological digs paints a rather more complex view of Emishi society.

Fortresses were built that acted as centres of Yamato culture and power. Chieftains of the Emishi were invited to court to offer small amounts of tribute and were rewarded with Imperial court titles.

The Emishi relied on horses in their warfare with the Yamato and using swift attacks managed to inflict defeats on the Yamato and their infantry-based armies. To ward off Emishi incursions into Yamato controlled territories the Japanese cultivated rivalries between the Emishi. This was known at court as the policy of "using barbarians to control barbarians." The Imperial armies also began to adopt tactics learned from the Emishi.

By the middle of the 9th century most Emishi lands were in the hands of the Japanese, though local Emishi chieftains remained important to governing the area. Having conquered the Emishi, the Japanese found some portions of their culture of value. The horse riding fighters developed from Emishi warfare would influence the later samurai.

TAKING HOKKAIDO

Ezo was the second largest island of the Japanese archipelago. This northern island remained outside of the control of the Japanese throne until relatively late in the history of Japan. It was only when settled by the Japanese that its name became Hokkaido.

Its native people, known as the Ainu, conducted trade with the Japanese for rice and iron in the 7th-13th centuries but maintained their ancestral way of life. In the 14th century a Japanese colony with centres of defence was constructed on the southern tip of Hokkaido. The Ainu resisted attempts by the Japanese to take over their land. In an uprising by the Ainu in 1457 one of their leaders named Koshamain attacked the Japanese settlement. He was slain in battle by Takeda Nobuhiro. Nobuhiro's decedents became the feudal lords of the south of Hokkaido.

The Japanese traded with the Ainu though rebellions continued to break out sporadically. The Japanese solidified their military presence on Hokkaido in response. Following the Meiji Restoration of the 19th century Hokkaido was taken into governmental control and prepared for widespread settlement by Japanese immigrants. Laws were passed in an attempt to force the Ainu to follow Japanese cultural norms.

ABOVE In Japanese art the Ainu people of Hokkaido were often depicted as barbarians in contrast to the more civilised Japanese

UNITING OF A NATION

OUTSIDE OF THE HEARTLANDS OF JAPAN, CONTROL OF A SOMETIMES FRACTIOUS PEOPLE HAD TO BE EXERTED CAREFULLY TO BIND THEM TOGETHER INTO ONE LAND

The seven circuits of the Gokishichidō system comprised dozens of different regions each with their own unique history, geography, and peoples. To bring all of them together under the rule of one emperor required a complete reformation of the nature of government. In the Asuka period the northern part of the Tōhoku region and Honshu island remained outside of the organisation of Japan into administrative districts and would have to be brought in later.

The five province and seven circuit system that divided Japan was made possible by the central authority of the emperors but also served to strengthen the role of the emperor. Reforms of the administration of the Japanese state proceeded from the 7th century onwards with the goal of bringing even regions far from the capital under Imperial control. Each of the seven circuits, known as dō, was composed of around ten provinces. Each of these provinces had an administrative centre which was the base of operations of a governor appointed by the emperor.

GOVERNING THE LAND

These governors managed both land belonging to the state, which was most of the agricultural land, and the royal estates. Royal estates were created in many provinces and their revenues were paid to the emperor. By having Imperial lands set up in a variety of places there was less chance of a local problem or rebellion cutting off the supplies of the court. These lands could also support an army if the emperor needed to dispatch one to anywhere in the country.

In the 7th century attempts were made to ensure that local disputes in the provinces could not escalate into wider uprisings. Weapons in all but the frontier provinces were gathered into storehouses, only to be issued to troops under Imperial control. This was designed to limit the power of clan chieftains who still held a great deal of authority in the provinces. Yet the emperor was not strong enough to rule without the cooperation of the people in the provinces.

The governors were instructed not to be high-handed with the people. They were not allowed to travel around with large entourages which would be costly for the local villages to maintain. If there was a difficult issue that had the risk of sparking trouble they were instructed to seek advice from the court rather than act on their own initiative. Everyone was granted the right to appeal - a decision which they felt to be unfair to an official higher up in the court.

The governor and other high ranking officials were generally drawn from the elite members of the court. Lower administrators were often recruited from the area. Local families could therefore aspire to Imperial favour in this way. While the governors and other people in high positions were rotated regularly between the provinces, those appointed from local communities held their positions for life which offered stability to the provinces, as well as loyalty from those appointed.

The management of the provinces followed a hierarchy that stretched all the way from the emperor in the capital to the individual worker in the fields. Because commoners were issued a plot of land to cultivate, censuses were instituted to share out the available land. When these were done groups of 50 households were placed together and from them a head-man was appointed whose task it was to oversee the planting of fields, payment of taxes, and suppression of crime.

ABOVE The station bells given to Imperial officials acted as a proof of identity and gave the bearer rights to withdraw supplies

STATION BELLS

Governing a country requires the ability to communicate orders from the centre of power to the periphery. To do this efficiently a series of roads were built stretching from the central provinces to the capitals of the seven circuits. To transmit Imperial decrees and other messages a series of post stations at regular intervals of 16km were created where messengers and other officials could find a change of horses and other aid they required for their journey.

To identify a person as having the right to take horses from a post station they were given a special station bell that proclaimed their rank. These bells were made of bronze and decorated with silk cords. Marks made on the side of the bell told the keepers of the post station how many horses you were allowed to withdraw for official use. The bells were quite large and heavy so the risk of a forged bell being used to steal horses was quite low.

The bells were issued to special messengers known as ekishi in the Asuka period and afterwards. As the central Imperial administration of Japan broke down in the 12th century other couriers were employed that relied on a military network and the station bells were abandoned.

To further bring the provinces within Imperial control, roads were constructed to join those in the seven circuits to those around the capital. Along these roads goods could flow to the capital and armies could move to any place needed to impose order. Tying provinces together occasionally had unintended consequences however. In 735 CE a smallpox epidemic began and in the next two years spread throughout all of the regions of Japan. Ease of transport of goods also made it easier for diseases to travel. In some areas a third of the population died. A centralised government was more able to respond to disasters such as this.

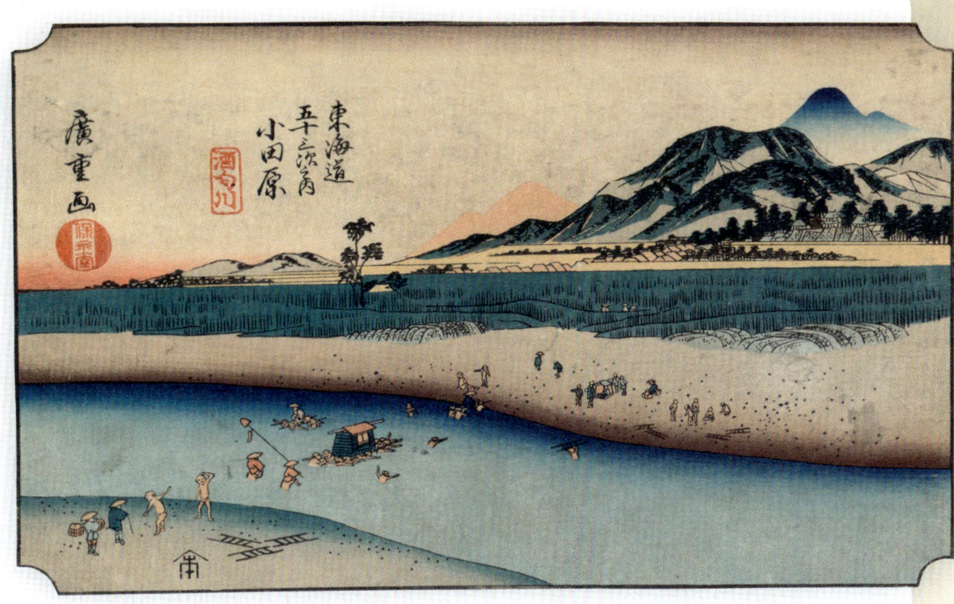

PROBLEMS IN THE PROVINCES

While the provinces offered increased strength through the resources they provided they could also be a source of potential weakness. In the 7th century, Japan became involved in wars with Korea and the Tang dynasty. Governors of the provinces were charged with raising armies and the risk of invasion from the sea meant that large, expensive defences had to be constructed allegedly causing widespread discontent.

Feudal lords called daimyo supplanted much of the emperor's control of the provinces. They ruled large private land-holdings called han which they used to create their own power bases. Japan had been created and organised, but it had not yet seen an end to struggles for control.

The bureaucratic organisation of the five province and seven circuit system helped to unify Japan into a single nation. The culture of the court was spread outwards through the layers of government to help create social structures that were recognised across the country.

But, while this system of provinces had a profound effect on Japan, it did not achieve the aim of total centralisation. There was a difference between the titular power of officials and the real power held by strong lords. Land which had been owned by the state began to be granted to important people and institutions, placing more control into individual clans. By the end of the 10th century the provincial system had mostly broken down. Half of all land was privately owned, and as private land was not taxed the revenues of the emperor dwindled.

"EACH OF THE SEVEN CIRCUITS, KNOWN AS DŌ, WAS COMPOSED OF AROUND TEN PROVINCES"

ABOVE The provinces of the seven circuits were vital to providing food supplies to the capital and brought in valuable resources

RIGHT The traditional division of Japan into provinces began in the Asuka period and expanded as more land was included in the area controlled by the emperor

THE AGE OF TRANQUILLITY

THE HEIAN PERIOD WAS A CULTURAL HIGH POINT OF JAPAN, BUT IT ALSO SAW SOME OF THE MOST VICIOUS STRUGGLES FOR CONTROL

The Heian period takes its name from the foundation of a new capital city founded by Emperor Kanmu in 794 CE. Disappointed by the rivalries and strife that had beset the Nara Period, the emperor decided that a new capital built on a Chinese model would bring stability. He also hoped that the absolute rule of the Chinese emperors could be emulated in Japan.

Heian-kyō - the "Capital of Peace and Tranquillity" - was set out in a grid pattern to further underscore the order Emperor Kanmu hoped to create. Better known today as Kyoto, this city would be the capital of Japan for 1,000 years. Despite the flourishing of Japanese culture during the Heian period, however, the hopes for peace and tranquillity were never quite achieved.

A NEW COURT

The new capital at Heian-kyō was a city of wide avenues and gorgeous buildings of red columns supporting green roof tiles. A palace complex was constructed to house both the personal living quarters of the imperial family and the administration buildings of the government. The palace was designed to be the centre of imperial power and a place where the struggles between nobles could be restrained. The strife caused by Buddhism was also excluded by having no Buddhist temples within the main area of the capital.

The physical construction of the new capital was matched by centralisation of the government of all Japan. While Emperor Kanmu ruled much of what is now Japan, there were still the Emishi people of the northern regions who were not under his direct control.

A Japanese text from the time describes how the Emishi were seen by those living in the capital. "In winter, they dwell in holes; in summer, they live in nests. Their clothing consists of furs, and they drink blood." Raids by both sides across the frontier presented a continued threat. The court's response was to push further into Emishi territory and construct forts to project their power. This was not a peaceful process.

The 38 Years' War against the Emishi had begun before Kanmu came to the throne. In 773, hostilities began with the Emishi rising up and destroying many of the Japanese fortresses in the region. The emperor of the time raised large national armies and sent them against the Emishi to limited success. Though the Japanese forces numbered in the tens of thousands, small bands of Emishi fighters were able to harry them and bring them to battle in unfavourable areas.

In the Battle of Koromo River in 789, 1,000 Emishi under the command of General Aterui beat a far more numerous Japanese force. Many Japanese warriors were drowned when they tried to flee. One Japanese general said: "Horse-and-bow warfare is learned from birth by the barbarians. Ten of our subjects cannot equal one of them." It became recognised that the National Army was no longer fit for modern warfare.

> "SMALL BANDS OF EMESHI FIGHTERS WERE ABLE TO HARRY THEM AND BRING THEM TO BATTLE"

Any Japanese male aged 20 to 59 could be conscripted into the national army as needed. A man would lay down his spade on the farm one day and pick up a pike the next. Around one month of every year was spent in service of the army. Putting down banditry was one of the army's main functions, but the service was open for abuse with some governors putting their conscripts to work on private farms. Nonetheless, against the quick-moving Emishi, these peasant soldiers were no match.

In a move that would have wide repercussions, Emperor Kanmu dissolved the National Army in 792. Forces would now be raised by local rulers, removing the expense of the army from the imperial throne. But it also loosened the emperor's grip on the warrior class.

The Emishi War ended in 811 with a nominal Japanese victory, but the Emishi of the northern areas remained independent. The real victory was for those who could afford to train as warriors. Suddenly being a trained warrior was a welcoming career opportunity for many

LEFT In building a new capital for Japan, Emperor Kanmu sought to reorder his empire and increase his control over fractious nobles

"FOR THE NEXT 170 YEARS, EVERY EMPEROR WAS BORN TO A FUJIWARA MOTHER"

noblemen. With limited official offices at the new court, and most of them in the hands of the Fujiwara clan, the ability to fight offered a path to influence. Service to an important lord was one of the only methods of movement up the social ladder. 'Bushi' was the name for any warrior, but those in service to a lord were called samurai.

A NEW ORDER

The Heian period saw a flourishing of Japanese culture. The design of the new capital had been made to resemble a Chinese imperial city, but the era saw a diminished Chinese influence. Diplomatic relationships with China ended after 838 CE as Japan no longer sought conquest abroad. Some trade continued and many Japanese scholars travelled in China to learn administration, but there were new routes to success in the court. Thousands of Chinese texts made their way to Japan, but Japan began to develop a unique literature of its own.

A form of Japanese writing developed that used Chinese characters to write out Japanese phonetically. From this, a true Japanese literature emerged. Works like *The Tale of Genji* and *The Pillow Book* offer the best insight into what life was like at the Heian court, and despite Emperor Kanmu's best efforts, the court remained a place of squabbles between high-ranking families and clans.

The pre-eminent family of the time was the Fujiwara. In past centuries, when a child ascended the throne, another member of the imperial family was chosen to act as their regent. This changed in 858 when Fujiwara no Yoshifusa was appointed sesshō (regent) for the young Emperor Seiwa. He was chosen because one of his daughters was consort to the previous emperor and he was grandfather to Seiwa. For the next 170 years, every emperor was born to a Fujiwara mother.

With the Fujiwara wielding so much power at court, many families felt shut out of imperial life. The Taira and Minamoto clans in particular had to find new ways of exerting influence. These two families were born out of a process known as Dynastic Shedding.

Even the large new palace and capital couldn't house all members of the imperial family; if an emperor found that he had too many sons, he could make them commoners by giving them surnames like Taira or Minamoto to ease the burden on the throne. By removing members of the imperial family in this way, the throne was secured for the emperor's chosen successor by removing potential rivals. The Taira clan could trace its origin to the younger sons of Emperor Kenmu, and later emperors. The abolition of the National Army offered a new path to these noble but unwanted children.

But the need for soldiers did not end just because the National Army was dissolved. Governors still required armed men to protect their lands from bandits. Tax collectors still needed protection from those who resented their presence. More and more, the court came to require warriors to put down rebellions.

When Taira no Masakado failed to find a career in court, he returned to his province in Shimōsa. There he became involved in political unrest and in 939 he raised a rebellion. Masakado conquered much of the Kanto region of Japan and declared himself Shinnō – The New

Emperor. At the same time, Fujiwara no Sumitomo led pirate raids in the Inland Sea. These warlords required putting down, but without an army of his own, the old emperor had to rely on other warlords to quell the revolts.

ABOVE LEFT The Battle of Dan-no-ura saw the end of the Genpei War, the destruction of the Taira clan and the ushering in of the Shogunate

ABOVE Emperor Go-Sanjō, shown here in retirement, broke the power of the Fujiwara and freed future emperors to act more decisively

The rebellions of Taira no Masakado and Fujiwara no Sumitomo were both put down with the aid of powerful lords. They revealed, though, that divisions between and within the clans were a serious threat to the throne. Members of the Taira and Minamoto could be found on both sides, and members of the Fujiwara who did not have a position or close blood ties to those at court could rise up. One way emperors sought to buy the loyalty of noble families was to grant them lands, but this was at best a short-sighted policy.

THE GREAT ESTATES

The population of Japan boomed in the Nara and Heian periods. Famine was a constant threat because of the small area of the country that was viable as farmland. But there was no incentive for farmers to clear wasteland and grow crops on it as any land they cleared could be claimed by the government. This changed in 723 when a law was issued that gave reclaimed land for three generations to the family who cultivated it. Later the grants were made perpetual. Suddenly wealthy families had an interest in clearing land to claim it for their own.

Great land estates were created in this way, but another system employed by the court ensured the loyalty of nobles. Land grants called shōen were made, turning over portions of the country to nobles and giving them power within their properties. Inside the shōen the government had no right to collect taxes, but the landowner could.

LADIES OF THE COURT

The outstanding artistic output of the Heian period is perhaps best exemplified in the female writers of the time. While most women were barred from official positions at court, many wealthy families gave their daughters an extensive education. With the development of written Japanese, many ladies began to pen their own works.

The Tale of Genji was written in the early 11th century by Murasaki Shikibu and many consider it to be one of the first great novels in all of literature. The tale follows a minor son of a Japanese emperor and his pursuit of a career, and it gives an intimate portrait of life at the Heian court.

Other writers penned zuihitsu, collections of essays and vignettes, that give a flavour of how court women lived at the time. In Sei Shōnagon's *The Pillow Book*, a lady-in-waiting to Empress Sadako records her thoughts in witty and amusing sections, and reveals the network of love affairs that riddled the court.

With writing being one of the few outlets for female creativity, it could spark rivalries. Murasaki Shikibu and Sei Shōnagon served different empresses and both sought to be the most famous writer of their day.

ABOVE *The Tale of Genji* vividly illustrates what life was like behind the scenes at the imperial court, especially for the women

By the 10th century, nearly half of the land was in the hands of private estates. These estates needed to be guarded and the owners turned to the samurai to protect their lands. The samurai warrior could expect to be paid in koku; one koku was the amount of rice it took to feed one man for a whole year - around 180 litres.

Shōen owners were powerful in their own domains. While there was a brass standard box held at the treasury that wooden payment boxes were supposed to be modelled on, in some shōen, owners used two different boxes. A larger one was used to measure out payments to the owners, while they used a smaller one to measure out their payments to others.

While land grants were distributed across the country, many magnates who owned the land spent most of their time in the capital to be near the court. Many areas were left to subordinates who could exploit the absence of their lord for personal enrichment. Samurai became important and powerful people in this power vacuum.

The shōen may have helped in the short term to buy loyalty, but they created more problems. As more shōen were granted, there was a decrease in the amount of imperial tax revenue and a reduction in the money the emperor could grant to courtiers. This led to courtiers wanting shōen of their own to support their station, which led to further decreases in tax revenue and more weakening of imperial power.

Families and factions also competed for the best and most productive lands. The Fujiwara family in particular was good at gaining territory for itself. One courtier lamented: "All the land in the country belongs to the regent's house. There is not even enough public land left to stand upon." Land was power because with more land, a lord could support more samurai. The power of the overmighty Fujiwara was finally checked, however, in the 11th century.

BREAKING THE FUJIWARA

At times during the Heian period, members of the Fujiwara were the de facto rulers of Japan. Emperors were invariably provided with a Fujiwara bride, and every emperor that came to the throne had a Fujiwara mother. When a child was seated on the throne, it was a Fujiwara who became sesshō, or regent. When the emperor grew up, the regent was often given the title of kampaku (chief advisor) and carried on ruling as before. Some Fujiwara regents deposed emperors who were still only in their thirties to ensure that they could have greater influence over the next to sit on the throne.

One Fujiwara, Fujiwara no Yorimichi, served as regent and kampaku for over 50 years through the reigns of three emperors. The last of these, Emperor Go-Reizei, had a Fujiwara mother and wife, but produced no male heirs. When Go-Reizei came to the throne, his half-brother Go-Sanjō was appointed as his heir. When he came to the throne after the death of his half-brother, Go-Sanjō was the first emperor in 170 years not to have had a Fujiwara mother.

While he was crown prince, Yorimichi was antagonistic towards the future emperor. He even refused him a sword traditionally given to the crown prince by claiming it only went to those of Fujiwara blood. Yorimichi is also said to have stopped Go-Reizei from abdicating, leading to Go-Sanjō being crown prince for 24 years.

When Go-Sanjō finally came to the throne, Yorimichi resigned as kampaku and was replaced by his brother Norimichi. Norimichi was sidelined by the emperor and the grip of the Fujiwara on power was reduced. Go-Sanjō filled his Private Office with scholars who had no ties of loyalty to the Fujiwara. Members of the Minamoto clan were appointed to high office. And although Go-Sanjō had a Fujiwara first wife, he did not name their son as his heir, instead waiting to see if he could produce a non-Fujiwara son with his second wife.

To further increase the power of the imperial throne, Emperor Go-Sanjō attempted to rein in the abuse of shōen. He declared all those granted since the accession of his predecessor were illegal and should be taken back into public hands. Any shōen that was a "hindrance" to the orderly running of the state was also liable to confiscation.

Minamoto officers were placed into the new Records Office that was charged with checking the paperwork for shōen and deciding whether they were legally granted or not. The land holdings of the Fujiwara, especially those in the family that had run the court, were diminished by the edicts of Go-Sanjō. This was partly because Yorimichi had been foolish enough to accept shōen lands simply by verbal agreement – leaving him with no records to protect his rights.

After just four years on the throne, Go-Sanjō abdicated in favour of his son, ensuring there could be no Fujiwara-chosen replacement. He would also be able rule alongside his son to make sure that he was not governed by the Fujiwara.

RIGHT The samurai emerged from the need for properly trained soldiers in the Emishi wars when the Japanese National Army was unable to beat its enemy

TOMOE GOZEN: A FEMALE SAMURAI

The samurai are generally depicted as warrior men, but there were examples of onna-bugeisha – warrior women. Many women from samurai families were trained in the use of weapons to help protect their families and homes in times of war, but some were also used on the battlefield.

In a 13th-century account of the Ganpei War, we are told of Tomoe Gozen, the female companion of Minamoto no Yoshinaka. "She was a remarkably strong archer, and as a swords-woman she was a warrior worth a thousand, ready to confront a demon or a god, mounted or on foot." When it came to the battles of the war, she was not simply a soldier. "Yoshinaka sent her out as his first captain... and she performed more deeds of valour than any of his other warriors."

Most onna-bugeisha were armed with a naginata, a pole tipped with a curved blade, but Tomoe Gozen was fitted out with the full kit of the samurai. One enemy leader attempted to drag her from her horse; Gozen decapitated him with her sword and delivered his head to Yoshinaka. Some historians have questioned whether Gozen was a real person, but her story has lived on and inspired generations of samurai.

RIGHT Tomoe Gozen is just one of the women in Japanese history to have taken up arms and led the life of a samurai

This was the beginning of cloistered rule - or insei - in the imperial system. Retired emperors would typically go to monasteries, but in reality they remained closely linked to the court. Go-Sanjō's son and successor Emperor Shirakawa followed his father's example and abdicated while young, but for the next four decades exerted powerful influence over his own son's reign.

The retired emperor had many advantages. He could remove himself from the intrigue of court and seek advice from hand-picked advisers. He was also freed from the complex ceremonies that were bound up with the throne.

There was a price to be paid for the system of cloistered rule, though. Power flowed away from the sitting emperor while the edicts of the retired emperor were of dubious legal authority. Sometimes a rapid turnover of rulers could leave several retired emperors all seeking to control the throne at the same time. Regional powers gained mastery of their own lands while the court was in conflict with itself.

THE COMING OF THE SHOGUNATE

Cloistered rule helped to bring about the end of the Heian period. In 1156, the retired Emperor Sutoku quarrelled with the reigning Emperor Go-Shirakawa over the imperial succession. Forces of Samurai from the Taira and Minamoto clans were called into the capital by both sides, but Go-Shirakawa emerged victorious. Sutoku was exiled and the last vestiges of Fujiwara power were finally destroyed. From then on, the Taira and Minamoto were the ones whose support an emperor would lean on.

Minamoto no Yoshitomo had led the winning forces, even killing his own father who was fighting on the opposite side, but it was Taira no Kiyomori who was rewarded with a powerful position at court by the Emperor. This led to a rivalry between the two. In 1159, Kiyomori left the capital for a pilgrimage. Yoshimoto rose up in rebellion, burned the palace, and captured the emperor. Kiyomori returned with an army of Samurai and freed the emperor.

The Genpei War of 1180-85 followed Taira no Kiyomori attempting to seat his grandson Antoku on the throne. The Minamoto clan rose in support of a rival claimant. After years of warfare, the Taira were driven from the capital, and they took their child emperor with them. The end of the civil war was at the naval Battle of Dan-no-ura. The Taira were utterly defeated. To save Antoku from capture, he was drowned by his grandmother. The Minamoto clan placed their chosen emperor on the throne.

Minamoto no Yoritomo, leader of his clan in the Genpei War, was give broad powers. He had control of taxation, the power to appoint ministers at every level, and was given the title ei-i Taishōgun. This was start of the shogunate that ruled from the city of Kamakura. As military dictator, Minamoto no Yoritomo ruled directly while the emperors in Heian-kyō became mere figureheads. Coming to power thanks to the actions of his samurai, there was now no illusion about where true power lay in Japan - it was on the edge of a samurai's blade.

RIGHT The Japanese portrayed the Emishi people as primitive barbarians - but often found themselves defeated by the Emishi

奉

2 将軍と武士

THE SHOGUN & THE SAMURAI

EMPEROR WITHDRAWS
CASTLES RISE LIKE RED-CROWNED CRANES
NEST FOR CENTURIES

TAIRA MASAKADO THE FIRST SAMURAI

AMONG THE SAMURAI, THERE WERE NONE LIKE THE FIRST, TAIRA MASAKADO, WHOSE PREMATURE REBELLION BROUGHT THE IMPERIAL COURT TO ITS KNEES

A shadow emerges from the flames, atop a horse. Digging his feet into the stirrups, he burns like a crazed dragon, over the corpses of his enemies and their houses. Before long, all of Japan will know the name of Taira Masakado, the greatest warrior in the realm, a New Emperor for a new era. And all of this could have been avoided.

Masakado was born in 903 CE, a great-grandson of Emperor Kammu, and a member of the powerful Taira clan. To ease the royal coffers, his grandfather, Prince Takamochi, renounced his royal lineage and settled in the eastern Kantō plain – the fertile lowland surrounding modern Tokyo – where his sons rapidly became powerful landowners. While the state had once held a monopoly on land, now most was privately owned – by temples, shrines, individuals and local clans.

Due to high imperial taxes, most peasants preferred to work for private landowners – who, with property disputes on the rise, armed them with spears and taught them archery, hunting and horse riding. Among the new class of private landowners were absent noblemen, living the high life in the capital of Heian, or modern Kyoto, retired governors who had settled in their former postings, and local clans with historic roots to their land. To make up for a lack of soft power, clans trained their peasants with exceptional bravado, promising to protect them at all costs, in return for absolute loyalty.

Before the samurai code of bushido – the way of the warrior – Japan referred to warfare as kyūba no michi, 'the way of the horse and bow' or kyusen no michi, 'the way of the bow and arrow'. Armies were centred around a core of mounted archers, drawn from prominent families, who maintained their own horses and equipment. They wore scaled armour, and though they carried swords, hand-to-hand combat was reserved for the peasants, armed with spears and shields. Local clan leaders could boast up to 500 peasants, giving special privileges to blood relatives and those whose families had served for generations. Before long, the country's mass of soldiers was concentrated in the hands of distant landowners, rather than the emperor. Despite this changing order, Masakado was raised to appreciate the prestige of imperial life. Boasting an honourable lineage, he spent his youth in the capital, a guard at the emperor's private residence, and even serving the future imperial regent, Fujiwara Tadahira. However, in spite of his immense promise, the young man failed to secure a good post. In 931 he decided to return to his homeland of Kantō – which had become a snake pit in his absence. With his father recently deceased, his uncles were keen to secure his land for themselves. Things came to a head when Masakado married his cousin against her father, Yoshikane's, wishes.

Sensing an opportunity, the powerful local warlord, Minamoto Mamoru, who had marriage ties to all of Masakado's uncles, sent his three sons to ambush him in the province of Hitachi in 935. Despite the element of surprise, they not only lost the battle, but their lives. Enraged by this unprovoked attack, Masakado rampaged across their lands, burning down their residences and the houses of hundreds of their supporters. Among the battle-dead was another of Masakado's powerful Taira uncles, Kunika. Though his death prompted his son, Sadamori, to return home from the capital, he lamented "Masakado is not my original foe". Sadamori had always been fond of his cousin – as fellow courtiers, they shared similar ambitions, and he had hoped to avoid conflict with him at all costs; perhaps even to ally with him.

In June 936, still bearing a grudge against his nephew, Yoshikane marched an army "as numerous as the clouds" to a fort in the southeastern district of Kazusa, linking up with his brother Yoshimasa. Senior clan leaders, they coerced Sadamori into joining their cause, leading a fresh-faced army of thousands, all clad in brand new armour and equipment, atop well-fed horses to Hitachi. There, Masakado lay in wait with a few hundred, poorly-equipped mounted soldiers and the 1,000-odd peasants he was able to muster. Against all odds,

RISE OF THE SAMURAI

Masakado's uprising marked the rise of the samurai warrior class

After Taira Masakado's death, members of the Minamoto and Taira clans – both stemming from the imperial family – continued to amass power. In 1028, another powerful Taira chieftain, Tadatsune, resigned as vice-governor of Kazusa and broke out in revolt, causing even more damage to the country than Masakado had – before surrendering to the powerful Minamoto Yorinobu, to whom the imperial court had appealed twice.

The Minamoto clan went on to play a crucial role in quashing the Early Nine Years War, defeating the rebellious Abe clan to the north, and again in the Three Years War against the Kiyowara family in the province of Mutsu. By the 12th century, the Taira and Minamoto clans had emerged as Japan's two greatest sources of military might, earning special privileges for their efforts. When tensions came to a head during the epic Genpei War of 1180-1185, the Minamoto emerged supreme, usurping power from the emperor and handing it to the clan leader, a military dictator, called the shogun.

Though the emperor remained a figurehead, this feudal society was ruled by the warrior class – the samurai – who served local lords in return for a food stipend, while their lords collected taxes and governed fiefs on behalf of the shogun.

Masakado routed the attackers, chasing Yoshikane to the provincial government headquarters in Shimotsuke. However, keen to avoid the scandal of killing a family member, he let his uncle go unscathed – instead reporting the unprovoked attack to the imperial government and his neighbours.

Months later, Masakado was summoned to the court, where he was handed a light punishment for arson – before being pardoned as a part of a general amnesty on New Year's Day in 937, when Emperor Suzaku came of age. Although he disavowed the life of war, no sooner had he returned home, the bitter Yoshikane launched another attack at the River Kogai. During the battle, he had his army raise images of Masakado's father and grandfather, supposedly to seek their protection, but most likely to deter his enemy from shooting arrows at his men. Having beaten Masakado, who was rendered immobile by sudden illness, he defeated him again at Toyota. Shell-shocked, Masakado and his family sought shelter among sympathetic clan members – but a traitor helped Yoshikane capture his wife and children.

Licking his wounds, after years of unprovoked assaults, Masakado had finally run out of patience. Raising an army, he marched on Hitachi, burning his uncle's residence to the ground, along with hundreds of

his supporters' houses. He chased Yoshikane into the mountains, destroying his crops along the way. Desperate, Yoshikane again bribed one of Masakado's men into betraying where his nephew slept and led a group of 80 warriors "each worth a thousand", to his camp. However, his nemesis was waiting for him, "with flaming eyes and clenched teeth". After a brief, explosive charge, half of Yoshikane's men lay dead. Broken, the Taira kingpin faded into obscurity, dying a few years later.

Although his troubles were far from over, Masakado had begun to develop something of a Robin Hood persona. When the controversial Prince Okiyo found himself at odds with the governor of Musahi, Masakado offered him shelter. Simultaneously, a local landowner, Fujiwara Haruaki, had developed a reputation for dodging his taxes - a man who official records said "behaved worse than barbarians or beasts". When the vice-governor put out a warrant for his arrest, Haruaki romped across Hitachi and Shimosa, robbing official granaries. As the region's constable, Masakado was ordered to arrest him, but instead offered him protection - claiming it his duty to protect the weak against the strong.

ABOVE LEFT Early Japanese bushidan were centred around elite mounted cavalry, practising 'the way of the horse and bow'

ABOVE In the 12th century, the Taira and Minamoto clans went to war, with the Minamoto emerging as the country's pre-eminent power

By June 939, Masakado's anti-authoritarian exploits had earned him an army of 1,000 mounted warriors, disenchanted with the established hierarchy. After defeating a large government army three times the size of his, Masakado seized the government's headquarters in Hitachi, before taking the provincial capital of Shimotsuke; along with its provincial seals and keys. Finally, after years of provocation, Masakado had broken out into full-blown rebellion. When Prince Okiyo pointed out that the punishment was equal whether he revolted in eight provinces or one, Masakado marched across Kantō - securing the entire region and appointing his own governors.

After supposedly consulting an oracle from Hachiman - the patron deity of war - Masakado did the unthinkable, declaring himself the 'New Emperor'. While his own brother admonished him for "acting without discretion" against the Mandate of Heaven, Masakado proclaimed, "Our age dictates that those who are victorious become rulers," before spitting, "your counsels are absolutely meaningless."

In January 940, he wrote to his former mentor, the regent Tadahira, justifying his actions, and claiming that his ambition lay only in Kantō. However, the court was understandably wary. During Masakado's uprising, further north, the previously 'pacified' Emishi people had broken out in revolt - destroying settlers' property. Simultaneously, an even greater rebellion had broken out west, under the leadership of the 'Pirate King' Fujiwara Sumitomo. Formerly the governor of

Iyo, on the southern island of Shikoku, Sumitomo had amassed a fleet of fishermen and petty seamen, and begun raiding the Inland Sea. Though the government offered him a senior post, he was not so easily appeased – instead capturing the vice-governor of Settsu, cutting off his ears, slitting his nose, murdering his son and taking his wife captive.

Terrified that the two had formed a secret, unholy alliance, the Heian court issued an edict demanding the eastern governors capture Masakado, with rewards of land and positions up for grabs, adding: "Since creation, this court has seen many rebellions, but none that compare to this." Highlighting its desperation, it held elaborate services and prayers, and ordered rituals be committed across the country by the mystic cults – to destroy Masakado through black magic.

At this juncture, as the country's greatest tsuwamono, or warrior, Masakado had amassed an army of 5,000 – joined by family members, landowners and those drawn to his martial prowess. In doing so, he had essentially created the first of many bushidan, or warrior bands.

Though the country had known insurrection, Masakado was no distant barbarian – he was of the finest stock, fighting among his own blood. In this dawn of civil war, his followers, and those of his rivals, began to create a new culture, away from the elegance of the Heian court. While warriors like Sadamori still used powdered foetus to treat battle wounds, they also developed new customs; announcing

BELOW After conquering Kantō, Masakado declared himself the New Emperor

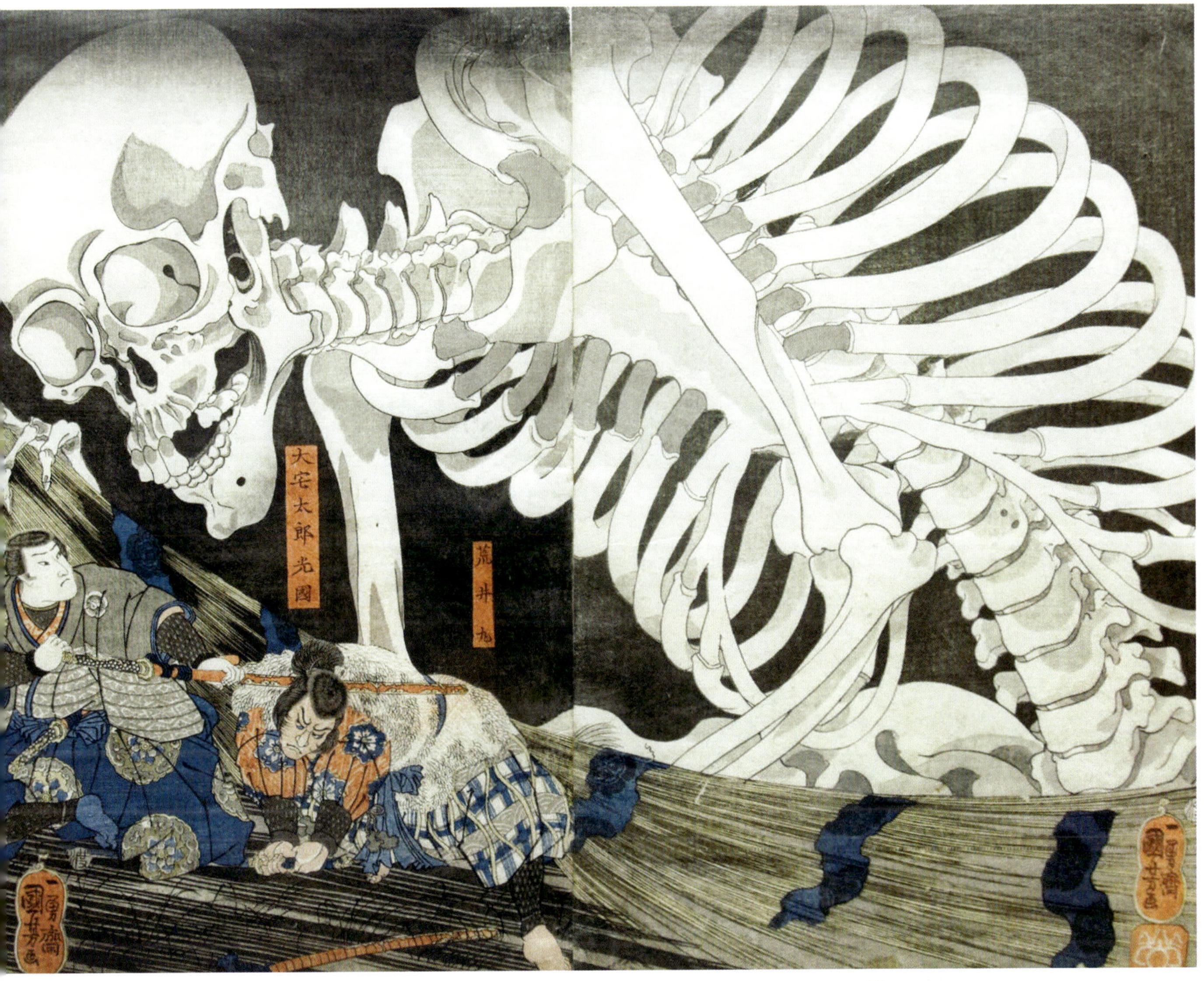

ABOVE In death, Masakado was immortalised - with Utagawa depicting his daughter, Takiyasha, summoning ghosts in a failed attempt to frighten her captors

their names with gusto, before rushing into battle. Similarly, they introduced the curved swords, lacquered ō-yoroi armour worn by commanders, and elaborate antlered helmets that would later become hallmarks of samurai warfare.

Having abandoned conscription, the imperial army had been made irrelevant by the new face of warfare. Instead, the court dealt out promotions, hoping to inspire private soldiers - like Minamoto Tsunemoto, the vice-governor of Musahi, Sadamori and Fujiwara Hidesato, the chief constable of Shimotsuke - to take matters into their own hands. While Sadamori had joined the war reluctantly, after Masakado's men captured and raped his wife, their hatred was now mutual.

Unfortunately for Masakado, despite his heritage, ability and prestige, he lacked the structural organisation that his spiritual samurai successors would later herald to great success. While he led an army of 5,000 across Hitachi to search for Sadamori, he was dependent on allies, rather than direct retainers. Even among family members, many fought out of self-interest, rather than personal loyalty. So, when Masakado returned home, with winter approaching, so too did his allies - leaving him with an army of just 1,000. After the chief constable Hidesato announced his allegiance with Sadamori, Masakado's men thoughtlessly launched a pre-emptive attack - only to be driven back in February 940. The vengeful Sadamori burned down Masakado's mansion, as well as the homes of his supporters, unleashing chaos in the ranks.

"THOUGH THE COUNTRY HAD KNOWN INSURRECTION, MASAKADO WAS NO DISTANT BARBARIAN"

芳年武者无類

相模次郎平将門

大蘇芳年

彫工 宗岡

The two sides picked the battleground of Kitayama in Shimosa for their last showdown. Though both erected walls of wooden shields, to protect them from cavalry charges, a violent gust of wind blew from behind Masakado, throwing his defences forwards, and hurtling Sadamori's back into his soldiers. With the defences down, the coalition's Fujiwara and Taira leaders launched a cavalry charge. Undeterred, Masakado hurled himself onto his horse and, with just 400 men, stormed into the enemy with such great ferocity, all but 300 fled. However, at this critical point, the wind turned against the New Emperor - and, as the enemy regrouped, he was hit by a stray arrow - killing him. Sadamori sent a lowly soldier to wrench his head from his body and took it to the capital, along with a certificate. Prince Okiyo was captured and killed just days later.

Meanwhile, the Pirate King Sumitomo, who had lost two chieftains and 2,500 men to bribes, was dealt a crushing blow after a turncoat surrendered to the government and led them to his base. Retreating to Kyushu, he sacked and raided all the way to Hakata, until he was eventually surrounded and killed.

With both rebels dead, the emperor visited the Kamo shrine and prayed for the dead - ally and enemy alike - at Enryakuji monastery on Mount Hiyei, overlooking the capital. Although peace had come, it had come at a high price. The nature of warfare, loyalty and rulership had been dealt a shocking blow - and though the emperor had won, it was not by the power of his state, but that of his provincial allies, and their private armies.

In the centuries to come, the Heian court blossomed into a centre of sophistication. Meanwhile, in the provinces, having cemented a stronger identity and honour code, the samurai would become the masters of Japan's emerging feudalist system. Though his rebellion was short-lived, Masakado was the harbinger of things to come, the personification of the new order. It was only a matter of time before the emperor lost his power; Masakado was simply 200 years too early. He left a legacy that would inspire the samurai for centuries to come: the idea that a warrior could be a courtly, educated man who followed his own moral code and valued his honour above all.

MASAKADO'S LEGACY

More than 1,000 years after his death, Japan still fears the wrath of Masakado

According to legend, after Masakado's head was cut off and put on show in the capital, it flew off by itself, in search of its body, before landing at Kubizuka or 'Head Hill' - in a fishing village at the heart of modern Tokyo, right next to the Imperial Palace. Superstition has since surrounded it.

After the Great Kantō Earthquake of 1923, when the Ministry of Finance attempted to replace the hill with an office building, 14 employees died, including the minister himself, and many others suffered ominous injuries. Then, in 1940, a lightning bolt sparked a fire adjacent to the hill, burning down nine government buildings - again, including the Ministry of Finance.

It was one of the few sites in the area to survive allied bombing in WWII and when the occupying forces tried to build over it, a bulldozer hit the foundation stone - killing its driver. Though he was declared an enemy of the emperor in 1874, Masakado was re-deified, by popular demand, in 1984 at Tokyo's Kanda shrine. To this day, companies in the area pay donations to Kubizuka, making employees go on pilgrimages to it, and laying out their offices in such a way that no one sits with their back to Masakado's grave.

ABOVE Masakado is enshrined at Tokyo's Kanda Myojin shrine, where he is revered, and feared, to this day as a patron deity

LEFT Before the samurai, Taira Masakado was the country's most renowned tsuwamono - a warrior, fighting with bow and arrow on horseback

RIGHT Every year, Fukushima residents take part in the Soma Nomaoi festival, a celebration of military exercises founded by Masakado

FEUDAL JAPAN

ŌNIN WAR
1467-1477

Due to controversy over who would succeed Ashikaga Yoshimasa, civil war breaks out. Yoshimasa originally names his brother as his chosen successor, however the unexpected birth of a son causes the family to fracture into two sides. Eventually it escalates into war, ending with no clear-cut winner.

DID YOU KNOW?

In the shogunate, the samurai (military nobility) had political power over the aristocracy

MINAMOTO YORITOMO BEGINS THE KAMAKURA PERIOD 1192

After winning the Genpei War (between the Taira and Minamoto clans) Minamoto Yoritomo establishes the feudal military government: the Kamakura shogunate.

WOKOU PIRATES BECOME RAMPANT 1350

Raids from pirates become particularly fierce. Attempts are made to fight back, including the Ōei invasion of 1419. General Zhu Wan becomes known for his fierce stance against the pirates.

SOUTHERN & NORTHERN COURTS REUNITED 1392

After being split between the Southern Court (four emperors who claimed sovereignty) and the Northern Court (six pretenders) an agreement is reached for reunification.

1192 — 1274 — 1333 — 1338 — 1457

KEMMU RESTORATION 1333

Emperor Go-Daigo restores imperial power, bringing back a civilian government after a century and a half of military rule. But this fails and is replaced with the Ashikaga shogunate.

JINNŌ SHŌTŌKI WRITTEN 1341

Kitabatake Chikafusa writes the *Jinnō Shōtōki*, mostly as an attempt to justify the importance of an emperor. This book formalises the transition from ruler to mystical symbol.

CONSTRUCTION OF EDO CASTLE
1457

A flatland castle built by Ōta Dōkan, it's one of the first foundations of what would become modern-day Tokyo.

FIRST MONGOL INVASION OF JAPAN 1274

Wishing Japan to become a vassal state, Kublai Khan dispatches emissaries requesting tribute. However, when the emissaries return time and time again empty handed the Khan declares war. The Mongolian army makes significant progress but is defeated with heavy losses at the Battle of Torikai-Gata. A second invasion is defeated in 1281.

MUROMACHI PERIOD 1338

Overthrowing the Kemmu Restoration, Ashikaga Takauji proclaims himself shōgun, beginning the Muromachi period. Takauji is known for his lack of fear, his mercy and generosity to those below him. In 1467, during the Ōnin War the shogunate has all but collapsed.

HONNŌ-JI INCIDENT 1582

At Honno-ji temple in Kyoto, Oda Nobunaga is surrounded only by officials and servants. The Akechi army marches on the temple in a coup. Unable to repel the attackers, Nobunaga commits suicide and his young page sets fire to the temple. Nobunaga's remains are never found.

DID YOU KNOW?

A samurai had to be prepared to commit seppuku - suicide by disembowelment with a sword

BATTLE OF MIYAJIMA 1551

In 1551 Sue Harukata rebels against his lord Ōuchi Yoshitaka. Mōri Motonari, a vassal of the Ōuchi clan, seeks vengeance and the two forces clash on the island Miyajima. The island is a shrine, with no birth or death allowed, and so is extensively cleansed afterwards.

BATTLE OF OKEHAZAMA 1560

Oda Nobunaga defeats Imagawa Yoshimoto and establishes himself as one of the leading warlords, with many samurai pledging allegiance to him.

INVASION OF KOREA 1592

Toyotomi Hideyoshi attempts to conquer the Korean Peninsula and China, however the invasion fails. A second invasion begins in 1597, but this too ends in failure.

BEGINNING OF THE EDO PERIOD 1603

Tokugawa Shogunate officially founds the Edo period following the Battle of Sekigahara in 1600, and takes three years to consolidate his power.

1543 — 1582 — 1603

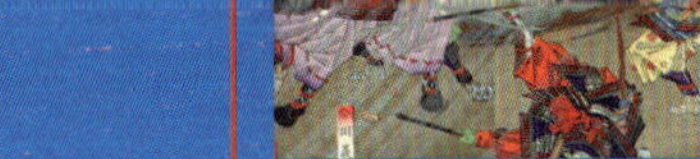

BATTLE OF YAMAZAKI 1582

Toyotomi Hideyoshi meets Akechi Mitsuhide (who rebelled against Oda Nobunga) in battle, having allied himself with the Mōri clan, and defeats him. Hideyoshi takes control.

INVASION OF SHIKOKU 1585

Toyotomi Hideyoshi invades the island of Shikoku, the smallest of Japan's main islands, and seizes it from rival warlord Chōsokabe Motochika.

SAN FELIPE INCIDENT 1596

The Spanish ship San Felipe is shipwrecked on the island of Shikoku. The Japanese accuse Christian missionaries in Japan of being 'fifth columnists' – 26 are crucified.

NANBAN TRADE 1543

The first Europeans arrive in Japan and establish a long-distance trade route. This begins with a group of Portuguese explorers, missionaries and merchants who introduce refined sugar, galleon-style ship building, Christianity and, of course, firearms.

CONSTRUCTION OF OSAKA CASTLE 1586

Toyotomi Hideyoshi commences the building of Ōsaka Castle. Modelled after his predecessor Oda Nobunaga's headquarters, Azuchi Castle, he seeks to surpass it. The castle features a five-storey main tower, with gold leaf on the sides. Having been reconstructed, it stands to this day.

THE WAR FOR JAPAN'S FUTURE

WHEN A POWER VACUUM LEFT JAPAN WITHOUT AN EMPEROR, TWO BROTHERS PREPARED TO FIGHT TO THE DEATH FOR THE ULTIMATE PRIZE

Toba closed his eyes and slowly inhaled the scent of the blossom swirling in the palace courtyard. In his younger years he would not have stopped to appreciate such a small pleasure, moved as he was by the ceaseless tides of power. But he was no longer young, and when one was confronted with a decision such as the one troubling his weary mind, the little fragments of peace that the gods deigned to offer seemed all the more precious.

His body had been failing him for some time, just as Konoe's had failed him, both brought low by the treachery of a fox lurking inside the royal coop. If only Konoe had been given more than his 16 years to sire an heir, a child that could have spared all this. But no, the gods had not seen fit to make Toba's final years easy. Japan required a new emperor, and Sutoku's progeny would likely be as trustworthy as his father. No, it had to be Shirikawa. Sutoku would have to accept that. For the good of the nation, Toba's favoured child had to sit the Chrysanthemum Throne.

THE PILLARS OF POWER

The fateful choice that faced the former emperor Toba shortly before his death in July 1156 was not without precedent. In imperial Japan, fathers often fashioned the destinies of their sons. Known as insei (cloistered or monasterial rule), a sitting emperor would abdicate the throne to be replaced by a son. However, this was no accession of power, as the 'cloistered' former emperor would continue to wield power from within the confines of a Buddhist monastery.

In 1107, Toba's meddling grandfather Shirakawa stepped aside for his son, yet offered him little say in the government of Japan, much to Toba's chagrin. Having married his son to a woman named Taikenmon-in, Shirakawa left him to stew in his own frustration until 1123, when he insisted Toba make way for his son Sutoku. Toba only did so begrudgingly (rumour had long claimed that it was in fact Shirakawa, and not Toba, who had fathered the infant emperor with the beguiling Taikenmon-in). However, Toba's days sulking in his grandfather's shadow would soon come to an end, and with Shirakawa's death came the influence that evaded Toba for so long.

Gripping the reins of power as Shirakawa had done, Toba ruled from behind the scenes. In 1142 he convinced Sutoku to move aside for his brother Konoe (Toba's eighth son). It would prove to be his first fateful manoeuvre.

Constantly sick, Konoe died in August 1155 at the age of just 16, leaving no heir behind. Assuming that his son would now ascend to the throne, Sutoku prepared to effectively replace Toba as the true power behind the new ruler of Japan. He was therefore apoplectic when news reached him that Toba intended to place his favoured son, and Sutoku's half-brother, Go-Shirakawa, in command of Japan.

For a time it appears that Sutoku's rage was held in check, for Go-Shirakawa ('Go' meaning 'later') ascended the throne without incident. And then, on 20 July 1156, Toba died. With the buffer between them removed, Sutoku immediately began scheming to overthrow his sibling and reclaim the crown. To do so, he would need the help of some influential allies.

THE EAR OF THE EMPEROR

For much of Japan's history, a clan known as the Fujiwara had enjoyed an intimate closeness with the country's emperors by marrying them to their daughters. However, upon the rise of Shirakawa (Toba's grandfather), these mighty regents had found themselves sidelined by a distrusting new ruler, setting the clan's ambitions back severely. Yet by the time of Konoe's death the Fujiwari, led by Tadazane, were once more in the ascendancy. In fact, in many ways they mirrored the imperial family in that Tadazane's sons both longed to become the clan's new leader.

TAMETOMO THE TERRIBLE

Not all war stories are about the victors – some tell the tales of power-hungry men

The eighth son of Minamoto no Tameyoshi, Tametomo earned a reputation as a ferocious warrior. Said to have been almost seven feet tall and heavily muscled, he was an awe-inspiring sight on the battlefield armed with his war bow. Impulsive and fearless, he assaulted several castles in Kyushu en route to mastering the island.

Having carved out his own kingdom, in 1156 Tametomo journeyed to Kyoto to support the former emperor Sutoku's bid for power alongside his father, Tameyoshi, who had disowned Tametomo when he was just 13 years old.

Equipped with a metre-long sword and a bow that took five men to string it, Tametomo battled valiantly, vowing to shoot his own brother if the chance arose. In the end, the lethal archer found himself on the losing side. Tortured and then exiled, he was initially left in peace. However, he couldn't resist his violent desires for long, and soon he was being hunted by a force backed with an imperial decree. Realising that his cause was utterly lost, Tametomo brutally murdered his nine-year-old son before plunging his blade into his stomach.

BELOW The Hōgon Rebellion, despite lasting just a few short hours, gave rise to the wider Heiji Rebellion soon after

Despite being the eldest, Fujiwara no Tadamachi was powerless to stop his father favouring his younger brother, Fujiwara no Yorinaga. Appalled at the prospect of Yorinaga seizing control, a desperate Tadamachi resorted to the most desperate of measures, informing a grief-stricken Toba that Konoe had been killed by Yorinaga (and not Tamamo-no-Mae, Toba's favourite courtesan) via an act of malicious sorcery, sticking pins into the eyes of a statue of the emperor in order to drain his life in reality. Evidently half mad with sorrow, Toba believed Tadamachi's wild claim, instantly devastating Yorinaga's prospects. It would be a betrayal he would remember.

CALL THE BANNERS

As well as the divisions within the imperial and Fujiwara families, splits were simultaneously opening among the kuge (aristocratic) clans. Yet arguably the most telling rift was the one pulling the families of Japan's most formidable entities apart: the Samurai.

The roots of the Minamoto and Taira Samurai clans lay in the cost-cutting policies of previous emperors. During the rule of Emperor Saga (809-23 CE), Japan's virile monarch had deemed it financially prudent to demote the majority of his 49 children to the position of nobles, thereby offloading the considerable burden of subsidising their privileged lifestyles. However, Saga wasn't so ruthless as to leave them with nothing, giving his shunned offspring the label 'Minamoto' (meaning 'origin') to signify that they shared the imperial lineage.

The Taira had emerged from a similar bout of child shedding when Japan's 50th emperor, Kanmu, demoted his grandsons. It was a move that would be mimicked by successive occupants of the Chrysanthemum Throne.

Despite rivalling each other for decades, by the time of Go-Shirakawa's rise to power, the leaders of the two Samurai clans found themselves back the same man: Sutoku. The ousted former emperor enjoyed the support of key figures in Fujiwara no Yorinaga, Minamoto no Tameyoshi, his son Tametomo (a legendary archer said to have once sunk a Taira ship with a single arrow) and Taira no Tadamasa. Yet while the loyalty of these seasoned dogs of war could be relied upon, the same could not be said of their ambitious pups, for behind Go-Shirakawa's bid to maintain power stood Minamoto no Yoshitoma (Tameyoshi's son) and Taira no Kiyomori (Tadamasa's nephew). The rebellious youngsters could count on the guidance of Fujiwara no Tadamachi, evidently still a supporter of Toba and his son dispute his lies about Konoe's death. But then treachery was rife in 12th-century Japan.

When the first drums of war had started beating, Minamoto Tameyoshi (previously expelled from the imperial court due to a mix of incompetence and an unhelpful habit of shielding criminals) had entrusted Yoshitomo with the recruitment of an army to aid Sutoku. Yoshitomo had fulfilled the task with enthusiasm – and then pledged the horde he'd amassed to Go-Shirakawa. Remarkably, once he'd spent sufficient time being comforted by his concubines, Tameyoshi asked another son to gather a fresh army. Fortunately for the

LEFT A scene from a scroll depicting the attack on Sanjō Palace

apparently exhausted Tameyoshi, this son remained loyal. Both sides now prepared to settle the dispute over the throne with blood and steel.

TO WAR

Tametomo stared blankly across the table at Yorinaga, a smug expression contorting the Fujiwara clansman's face. It had seemed only moments ago that the rest of the war party backed Tametomo's proposal for a nocturnal assault on Go-Shirakawa's palace. Then Yorinaga intervened in his high-handed way to dismiss the notion as dishonourable. Meanwhile, in an identical meeting held inside Go-Shirakawa's stronghold, Yoshitomo, sharing his brother's martial intelligence, made the same suggestion. The emperor's war party immediately sanctioned it.

Riding at the head of 600 cavalrymen (each one accompanied by two foot soldiers), Yoshitomo and Kiyomoro rode to the enemy's palace in Kyoto under the cover of darkness.

The men watching the palace walls would not have appreciated the threat they faced until the first arrows began thumping into flesh and wood. As they scrambled to return fire (led by the valiant Tametomo, who is believed to have been able to draw a bow further than any other man due to his left arm being several inches longer than his right), Kiyomori threw his forces at the west gate of the compound. A fierce struggle ensued as Sutoku's much smaller force fought back. Eventually, under a rain of arrows, Kiyomori was forced back. Yoshitomo then suffered the same fate.

As the battle raged, a contingent of Go-Shirakawa's troops penetrated the palace defences and set the compound ablaze. Shielding their eyes from the flames, Sutoku's men had little choice but to flee. Go-Shirakawa had managed to emerge victorious.

> "BOTH SIDES NOW PREPARED TO SETTLE THE DISPUTE OVER THE THRONE WITH BLOOD AND STEEL"

The cost of rebellion proved to be extortionate for the men who had supported Sutoku. Fujiwara no Yorinaga had perished from an arrow wound shortly after the battle. Tameyoshi and Tadamasa were both executed, their son and nephew respectively - but reluctantly - giving the orders. Tametomo suffered having the tendons in his bow arm severed before being cast into the wilderness, where he committed the first recorded act of seppuku (harakiri) - suicide by disembowelment. As for Sutoku, he was banished to Sanuki Province, where he is said to have died and become an evil ghost hell-bent on revenge.

His enemies dead or scattered, Go-Shirakawa quickly mopped up the remnants of Sutoku's army. By way of thanks, he promoted Yoshitoma to Provisional Head of the Left House (imperial) Guards. Kiyomori fared even better, elevated as he was to the post of governor of Harima

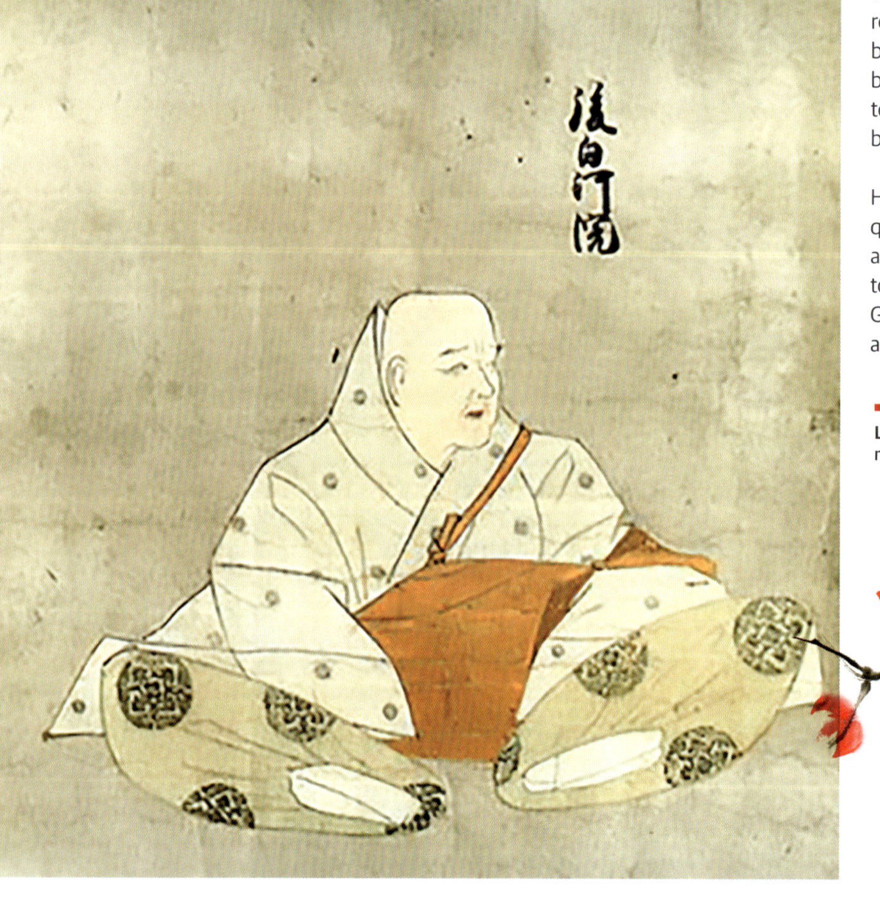

LEFT Emperor Go-Shirakawa was Japan's last absolute monarch before the shogunate

Province. Go-Shirakawa had every right to be pleased, but unbeknown to the emperor, his generosity had in fact sowed the seeds of further bloodshed. By thanking the Minamoto and Taira clans in such unbalanced fashion, he'd unwittingly set them on a path to war.

THE HEIJI REBELLION

On 5 September 1158, Go-Shirakawa abdicated his throne to make way for his son Nijō. As was custom, the cloistered emperor remained in charge. Even so, the presence of a 15-year-old boy on the throne may have emboldened the Minamoto clan, for when Taira no Kiyomori embarked on a pilgrimage the following year, they wasted no time in pouncing on the opportunity before them. In league with Fujiwara no Nobuyori, Minamoto no Yoshitomo laid siege to Sanjō Palace in Kyoto, placing Go-Shirakawa and Nijō under house arrest. For good measure, they torched the palace and murdered Nijō's retainer (a royal attendant), Fujiwara no Michinori. Nobuyori even had the audacity to proclaim himself as imperial chancellor. But the pair hadn't reckoned on Kiyomori's swift return.

Upon reaching Kyoto, Kiyomori confronted the unfolding crisis with his usual calm, offering Nobuyori pretend peace terms. While the hubristic new chancellor prevaricated Kiyomori engineered Nijō and his father's escape. With the emperor now safe, Kiyomori commanded his eldest son, Shigemori, to finish the rebels. He duly led 3,000 cavalry in an all-out assault on the palace.

Unsurprisingly, Nobuyori fled at the first hint of a struggle. Fortunately for Yoshitomo, his son Yoshihira fought back, pursuing Shigemori through the corridors of a now blazing palace while the Samurai sons duelled a savage battle raged beyond the walls. As both sides slashed and shot at each other, Kiyomori effected a feigned withdrawal in order to lure the Minamoto soldier out into the open. His ploy worked, allowing a detachment of Taira troops to occupy the royal compound. Cut off, the Minamoto rushed Kiyomori's position but were beaten back. Their lines soon buckled as panicked men quit the field.

Yoshitomo died likewise, making it as far as Owari Province before his retainer tired of his company and killed him while he was taking a bath. Two of Yoshitomo's sons followed him into the afterlife, including Yoshihira, but three were spared, among them a boy named Yoritomo, who, 25 years later, would establish the Kamakura shogunate, the first to rule Japan. Minamoto territories and wealth were snatched by a vengeful Kiyomori, who then formed the country's first samurai-dominated government.

The legacy of the Heiji disturbance was far more important in determining Japan's trajectory than the event itself. A simmering rivalry between the two most formidable Samurai clans had boiled over once more into open war, and it wouldn't be for the last time.

In 1180 the clans would clash again in the Genpei War, a conflict that would result in one dynasty standing on the ashes of the other and change the way in which Japan was ruled for centuries. Only one thing was certain in the wake of the Heiji rebellion: Japan would know no peace.

THE NINE-TAILED FOX

Uncover the story of Tamamo-no-Mae

When a couple walking through a woodland stumbled upon a baby girl wrapped in swaddling, they immediately resolved to take her home and raise her as their own. It wasn't long before they realised that she was no normal child. Blessed with a razor wit and the ability to read advanced texts at a rapacious speed, young Tamamo-no-Mae earned the right to recite poetry before Emperor Konoe. Fascinated by the child, he made her an imperial servant.

In time she blossomed into a beautiful, charming young woman, one able to pass any scholarly test. Besotted, Konoe promoted Tamamo-no-Mae to the role of his consort, spending every free moment with her. And then he fell gravely ill.

Desperate to save the young emperor, imperial servants summoned a priest to pray for his recovery, but to no avail. Increasingly frantic, they resorted to hiring a sorcerer to uncover the truth. It didn't take long for the spell weaver to point the finger of blame at Konoe's consort. When Tamamo-no-Mae inevitably denied any involvement, the sorcerer insisted that she partake in a holy ritual. No evil spirit could hope to survive it.

However, initially everything went well, with Tamamo-no-Mae remaining unchanged. Suddenly, a tail sprouted from her rear, followed by another, and another, until nine red tails shimmered behind her. Exposed as a fox-like demon, she fled, only to be hunted down by the emperor's men and shot. As she lay dying, her spirit passed into a boulder called sessho-seki (the killing stone). To touch it was fatal. Here she remained until a passing monk heard her cries and listened to her confession, upon which he released her. As one of the three evil yōkai (ghosts) of Japanese myth, her soul still stalks the wilderness to this day.

A NEW POWER RISES

AN AMBITIOUS YOUNG MAN PICKED UP A BLOODIED GAUNTLET AND REJUVENATED A NATIONAL STRUGGLE THAT WOULD RESULT IN THE ANNIHILATION OF ONE OF JAPAN'S MOST FORMIDABLE FAMILIES

To understand why the Genpei War of 1180–1185 erupted into a conflagration that would claim thousands of lives and alter the course of Japan, one must first sift through the embers of an uprising that occurred 20 years earlier.

Eager to snatch power from the Taira-backed Emperor Nijo and his predecessor, the retired emperor Go-Shirakawa, the Minamoto clan were gifted the ideal opportunity to overthrow Japan's ruler in January 1159 when Taira No Kiyomori, leader of the Taira clan, departed the city of Heian-Kyō (Kyoto). However, their planning lacked forethought, the Minamoto leadership, spearheaded by Minamoto No Yoshitomo, giving little consideration as to how they would defend the city upon Kiyomoro's return.

After placing Go-Shirakawa and the emperor under house arrest and setting the imperial palace ablaze, all the Minamoto could do was wait. Their fate would be delivered just weeks later when Kiyomori's forces lured the Minamoto out of the city and routed them.

Owing his life to Kiyomori, in 1167 Go-Shirakawa (the real power behind the throne) promoted his saviour to the role of Daijō-daijin (chancellor), the highest office in the land, having smoothed the path to the top for Kiyomori since the rebellion six years earlier. As astute in the confines of the imperial court as he was on the battlefield, Kiyomori wasted little time in installing his loyalists in prominent positions and executing or banishing any conspirators harbouring dreams of toppling him. However, he wasn't solely focused on domestic issues and worked to establish lucrative trade links with Song China.

ABOVE This stunning artwork depicts the total destruction of the Taira clan at the Battle of Dan-no-ura

Despite being secure in his position as the most formidable leader in the country, Kiyomori further consolidated his grip on power in 1171 when he arranged for his daughter to wed Emperor Takakura. The couple would welcome a son in 1178, and the year after his arrival Kiyomori launched a daring coup, sweeping his rivals from office and placing Go-Shirakawa under house arrest. He then added insult to injury in 1180 by crowning his two-year-old grandson Emperor Antoku. It seemed that only the skies now eluded the hands of Kiyomori, but he had in fact made a critical error two decades earlier that would come back to haunt him.

BROTHERS IN ARMS

In the wake of the failed Heiji Rebellion, its leader, Minamoto No Yoshitomo, had suffered the inglorious end of being executed while in the bath, and as was the custom when dealing with rebels, two of his sons, Yoshihira and Nobuyori, were also put to death. Three of his other sons, Minamoto no Yoritomo, Minamoto no Yoshitsune and Minamoto no Noriyori, were set to receive the same fate only (according to some accounts) to be saved when their pleading stepmother appealed to Kiyomori's better nature. In a rare display of mercy, Kiyomori agreed to exile the siblings, sending Yoritomo to Izu Province in the south while banishing his brothers to other parts of the country.

By sending Yoritomo to live with the Hōjō clan (a branch of the Taira), Kiyomori must have assumed that he had rid himself of a problem. After all, what harm could a young boy do, especially with a loyal ally in the form of Hōjō Tokimasa watching over him? Unfortunately for Kiyomori, he hadn't accounted for true love.

Tokimasa was the proud father of 15 children, including a daughter named Hōjō Masako, who happened to fall in love with Yoritomo. After initially refusing the two his blessing, Tokimasa acquiesced and permitted them to marry. Yet while this arrangement threatened to enrage Kiyomori, it didn't amount to a direct threat to his rule. That would come in 1180.

Having upset the nobility by muscling his way to the top only to then imprison the former emperor who helped him to climb the ladder, Kiyomori had plenty of opponents at court, but his list of adversaries didn't end there. Tired of a capital in Taira hands that demanded taxes and offered little in return, the masses were becoming agitated, including the country's Buddhists, angered by measures that suppressed their rights.

On top of all this, an influx of Chinese currency had sparked terrible inflation. All the ingredients for a revolt were therefore in place, and in 1180, Prince Mochihito, himself aggrieved at being overlooked for the throne, issued a call to arms alongside a member of the Minamoto clan named Yorimasa. What would come to be known as the Genpei War had begun.

A CLASH OF CLANS

This brutal conflict would be chronicled approximately 150 years later in the Heike Monogatari (The Tale of the Heike), and it would start with a devastating defeat for the men who triggered it. After being pursued by Taira forces, on 20 June 1180 Mochihito and Yorimasa's army crossed the Uji River outside Kyoto and then destroyed the bridge they had marched across to frustrate the Taira.

Undeterred by the prospect of getting wet, the Taira stormed across the river and demolished the rebels. Yorimasa, watching on as his brave sons fought against the tide, committed seppuku (ritual suicide). As for Mochihito, the grandson of Go-Shirakawa was apprehended shortly after the battle and promptly killed. To the routed Minamoto troops fleeing into the surrounding hills, any hope of overthrowing Kiyomori appeared dead. But there was still a young man with dreams of achieving what the recently massacred rebels couldn't, and for Minamoto no Yoritomo the situation was personal.

Driven by his loathing of the man who had overseen the ruination of his clan, Yoritomo stepped up to lead the Minamoto and vowed to continue the fight. Upon hearing word of his declaration, Noriyori and Yoshitsune raced to join their brother, whose cause was further backed by his father-in-law and a cousin named Kiso Yoshinaka. It wasn't long before warriors across the land were rallying to Yoritomo, and even an early defeat to a Taira-supporting army didn't extinguish the fire inside the former exile.

After taking control of Izu Province, Yoritomo set about establishing a new warrior state in the Kanto region (located in the centre of Honshu), a territory seething with samurai who revelled in battling the elites. Offered the chance to govern themselves without interference

LEFT A ruthless operator, Minamoto no Yoritomo ordered the executions of both a future son-in-law and the baby of a concubine he had impregnated

ABOVE From a cliff-top vantage point Yoshitsune inspects a Taira stronghold. Still hailed as a hero today, he overshadowed his brother Noriyori

from the capital, these warriors helped Yoritomo to construct a coastal stronghold in Kamakura and capture every government headquarters in Kanto. In time Kamakura would flourish into just the third city in Japan, the others being Kyoto and Hiraizumi in the north.

The nation was now divided into opposing East and West sections, but before hostilities could resume, famine intervened, preventing Kiyomori from dispatching a force to Kanto until November. Depleted by desertions, by the time this host reached Fujikawa beneath the slopes of Mount Fuji it only numbered 4,000. Severely outnumbered, the Taira troops settled down for the night, but as they milled around their camp they noticed small fires springing up throughout the surrounding hills. Convinced that they were warming a vast Minamoto army, the Taira started to panic, and when a flock of waterfowl were spooked and flew over their camp the Taira feared that the racket was in fact the beat of a million hooves. Glancing over their shoulders at a cavalry charge that never came, the Taira rode for home.

At the same time as this embarrassing reversal, Kiso Yoshinaka was making progress in Shinano Province to the north of Kanto, whipping up the locals with the help of a female samurai named Tomoe Gozen. Revolution filled the air as various factions across Japan fought to oust their Taira overlords.

By 1181 Kiyomori, already frustrated in battle and at court by pro-Minamoto bureaucrats, was confronted with uprisings in Owari, Omi and Mino (endangering grain supplies), and Kyushu, severing his links to China. Even the monks were up in arms. It all proved too much for Kiyomori, who fell ill and died that same year. With his first son dead, power was placed into the incompetent hands of another - Munemori. Or was it?

Desperate for a male heir, Kiyomori had been elated in 1147 when his wife gave birth to a son. However, some accounts claim that she in fact bore a daughter. Frantic, she allegedly swapped the baby girl for the infant son of an umbrella salesman and then passed the boy (Munemori) off as Kiyomori's legitimate son. While this may sound fanciful, it would at least explain why Munemori was the exact opposite of his 'father'.

As well as inheriting control of half of Japan and a war to fight, Munemori also had to contend with the Yōwa Famine, which was triggered by drought and would last until 1182. Bodies littered the streets, and the starving capital turned to the provinces for food, further exacerbating the situation elsewhere. Not one to let a good famine go to waste, in the east Yoritomo made further gains by promising people food in return for land, and he even had the audacity to write to the capital to suggest that he be acknowledged as the ruler of the east of Japan.

"DRIVEN BY HIS LOATHING OF THE MAN WHO HAD OVERSEEN THE RUINATION OF HIS CLAN, YORITOMO STEPPED UP TO LEAD THE MINAMOTO"

Munemori, his ambitions already frustrated by Kiso and Tomoe Gozen (the latter taking the heads of seven mounted enemy soldiers in one battle), rebuffed Yoritomo's offer, and when the famine subsided in 1183 he renewed his efforts to finish Kiso off once and for all.

Leaving Kyoto on 10 May, the Taira army, which numbered around 40,000, marched for the passes that link western Honshu to the east. At the start of June they sighted Kiso's forces (approximately 5,000 men) in Kurikara Pass. Confident of victory, the Taira descended into Jigokudani (Hell Valley), where they encountered a sea of enemy banners that indicated a far larger Minamoto army. In truth, Kiso was stalling for time while a detachment of his troops snuck around to the rear of the Taira.

After a routine exchange of arrows and a series of duels between individual samurai, at sunset the Taira discovered to their horror that they were in fact completely trapped. But that was only the start of their troubles. A chorus of snorts and the sound of hooves scraping at the stony ground floated down the valley, shortly followed by a stampede of oxen with flaming torches fastened to their horns. The Taira were quite literally swept off the valley path to their doom.

FAMILIAL FRICTION

The momentum of the war now shifted irreversibly in favour of the Minamoto. Yet all was not tranquil among the clan leaders. Seeking to capitalise on his crushing victory, Kiso seized the capital (Emperor Antoku was whisked away to safety just in time). Yoritomo viewed this as an intolerable threat to his rule and ordered his brothers to reclaim Kyoto. Meanwhile, Yoritomo schemed with Go-Shirakawa and succeeded in convincing the government to recognise Kanto's independence. Although an unprecedented feat in itself, this arguably was the secondary prize given that Yoritomo was also afforded the right to police Japan.

For his part, Kiso pressurised the court into naming him Seii Taishogun ('barbarian-conquering generalissimo'), a title formerly reserved for those leading troops north to battle the Emishi ('shrimp barbarians'). This after he had butchered an underground resistance movement, narrowly avoided the attentions of an assassin sent by Yoritomo, torched Go-Shirakawa's palace and ordered him arrested once again.

Come February 1184, Kiso was as welcome in the capital as an outbreak of smallpox, and his demise finally came at the Battle of Awazu in Omi Province. Far more dangerous in battle than politics, Kiso and his valiant comrade Tomoe Gozen acquitted themselves well, but ultimately numbers told, and the courageous duo were forced to mount a final stand. In a display of galling ingratitude, Kiso ordered Gozen to flee – not because he cared for her safety, but because he couldn't countenance the indignity of perishing beside a woman. No doubt offended, Gozen took her frustrations out on a formidable enemy soldier. Legend has it that she coolly sliced off his head before removing her armour and riding off never to be seen again.

As for Kiso, an arrow to the face permanently punctured his dreams. Upon witnessing his lord's death, Imai Kanehira, Kiso's foster brother, bit down on the tip of his sword and dived from his horse in what must rank as one of the most dramatic suicides ever committed. To remove any doubt as to who now held Japan, Yoshitsune paraded Kiso's head in front of the imperial court. An order was then passed condemning all Taira loyalists to the same fate.

What remained of the Taira moved west to familiar ground from where they could utilise their traditional naval strength on the Inland Sea. They were harassed all the way by Yoritomo's brothers, who assaulted a fort in Ichinotani, forcing Munemori and the infant Emperor Antoku to escape on a ship.

ABOVE Renowned for collecting the heads of her enemies, Tomoe Gozen sliced her way into history before vanishing

Pressed even further west, the Taira barricaded themselves inside a second fortress on the island of Kojima. Surrounded by sea water, it posed an almost impregnable obstacle, but sometimes no wall can repel local knowledge. Eager to please the advancing Minamoto army, a fisherman revealed that at low tide a path to the fort would appear. He was thanked for his advice and then skewered. As Noriyori tore down the defences of Kojima, Yoshitsune received several vessels sent by Yoritomo, which he used to sail across the sea and attack Yashima, another Taira stronghold. Munemori fled again, but now the Taira were forced all the way down to Hikoshima on the tip of Honshu.

Cobbling his own fleet together (at the time Japanese boats resembled flat rafts), Noriyori sailed his troops over to Kyushu, nearby to where the last remaining Taira holdout stood. Yoshitsune witnessed his own fledgling navy swell into an armada, and he soon made for the Taira bottled up in the Shimonoseki Straits.

DOOM OF THE TAIRA

The Battle of Dan-no-ura on 25 April 1185 pitted between 700 and 840 Minamoto 'ships' against a Taira fleet of 500. Desperate to protect their emperor, the Taira hid Antoku in a small boat while an elaborately decorated imperial vessel acted as a decoy.

A hail of arrows preceded the fleets colliding. Warriors on both sides cut their way onto enemy boats and engaged in merciless duels. One samurai sliced his way towards Yoshitsune, who, despite his ability with a blade, leapt to another boat. Infuriated at being denied the chance to kill a key Minamoto leader, the samurai booted one man overboard before placing two others in a headlock and diving beneath the waves. Men fought and died for several hours in a tight contest. And then the tide turned against the Taira. Literally.

As the water shifted beneath the armies, so too did the momentum above the surface when a traitor named Taguchi Shigeyoshi turned his men on the Taira and informed the Minamoto of Antoku's true whereabouts. Poor Antoku soon found his boat assailed by screaming samurai. No doubt terrified, his situation worsened when his grandmother snatched him up in her arms along with the imperial sword and jewel and sent them all to a watery grave. The imperial mirror was spared and the jewel later recovered, but like the sword, Taira hopes were fatally sunk.

In a fittingly dramatic end, the Taira leaders tied themselves to anchors and followed their emperor. Munemori, while contemplating a similar end, was knocked overboard. He was later fished out and put to death. To this day locals say the crabs of the bay bear the faces of the dead Taira on their stomachs.

LORD OF JAPAN

His enemies slaughtered and his clan restored to its former glory, Minamoto no Yoritomo stood as the supreme ruler of Japan. Supreme, but not undisputed, for Go-Shirakawa backed Yoshitsune in the imperial court, perhaps hoping that he would act as a check on Yoritomo. He was mistaken.

After escaping Kyoto and travelling to the northern capital of Hiraizumi, which he reached in 1187, Yoshitsune was taken in by the Oshu Fujiwara clan. No doubt exhausted and not a little concerned by his elder brother's demands that he be returned to the south, Yoshitsune probably felt rather relieved to have found sanctuary. That is until the leader of the clan protecting him, Fujiwara no Yasuhira, buckled and ordered Yoshitsune to kill himself. The unfortunate warrior's head was sent to his brother as proof.

Yasuhira may well have anticipated a sign of Yoritomo's appreciation, but he had in fact gravely offended the war lord. Yoritomo burnt Hiraizumi to the ground. Yasuhira attempted to escape but was betrayed and murdered. His head was also sent to Yoritomo who, true to form, ordered the execution of the traitor who dared to kill his own lord.

Noriyori managed to evade his brother's wrath until 1193, when he was killed after offering to care for Yoritomo's wife Masako in the wake of false rumours of Yoritomo's death.

A year before Noriyori's unjust execution, the imperial court bestowed the title of Seii Taishogun ('commander-in-chief of Japan') upon Yoritomo, thereby giving rise to the first shogunate ever to rule the country. By elevating Yoritomo to such prominence the court was simultaneously transforming the role of emperor into a mere figurehead.

Yoritomo only got to enjoy the role of shogun for seven years. In 1199 he died a rather unbefitting death when he fell off his horse. He was succeeded by his son Yoriie, a self-obsessed brat who almost sparked a civil war when he tried to snatch a samurai's concubine. However, his mother Masako didn't approve of Yoriie's promotion and forced him to relinquish the shogunate in place of his younger brother Sanetomo, thereby (quite ironically) turning the Kamakura Shogunate (1185-1333) into a sort of figurehead government while the Hōjō clan pulled the strings. Masako's machinations ensured that Kamakura remained as the real centre of power in Japan.

RIGHT Located on the island of Miyajima, in Hiroshima Bay, this statue commemorates the great Taira no Kiyomori

THE NUN SHOGUN

Born into the Hōjō clan in 1157, Hōjō Masako was destined for the top. Legend has it that when she was 20, Minamoto no Yoritomo penned a love letter intended for Masako's sister. In a twist of fate the samurai charged with delivering it mistakenly handed the note to Masako. Shortly afterwards, Masako's sister is said to have dreamt that she held the sun and moon in her hands. Spotting an opportunity, Masako told her that this vision was a bad omen and offered to buy the dream from her in exchange for a kosode (a short-sleeved garment).

ABOVE Hōjō Masako played a key role in government right up until her death in 1225 at the age of 69

In reality, Masako knew that this dream spelled good fortune, and after running away to live with Yoritomo in a mountain temple because her father forbade them to marry, Masako was permitted to wed her true love. In time the couple would rule the east of Japan from Kamakura. But she didn't have it all her own way.

Forced to hand her son Yoriie over to the Hiki clan as part of the menoto tradition that saw families adopt the elite's offspring and raise them as their own, Masako then discovered that Yoritomo had not remained faithful while she had been away giving birth. Understandably upset, she ordered a samurai to burn down the house of her husband's lover. When he strayed again by impregnating a lady-in-waiting, Masako threatened to have the baby killed.

It would be unfair to say that she was acting out of line, as Japanese culture openly acknowledged a scorned wife's right to take revenge in a custom known as uwanari uchi.

After Yoritomo's death, Masako became a nun, but that didn't spell the end of her political endeavours. Quite the opposite. By removing Yoriie (with whom she had never been given the chance to bond) as shogun and entrusting power to another of her children, Masako was making sure that the Kamakura Shogunate survived the upheaval of its founder's demise.

SECRET POWER BEHIND THE SHOGUN: THE HŌJŌ CLAN

THROUGH WILLPOWER AND SOME GOOD FORTUNE, THIS FAMILY BECAME THE MOST POWERFUL CLAN IN ALL OF JAPAN

After decades of conflict over the rule of Japan, in 1180, the Genpei War broke out between the Taira and Minamoto clans. The war would last until 1185 when the Minamoto clan won, establishing a new feudal military government known as the Kamakura Shogunate. The leader of the Minamoto clan was Minamoto no Yoritomo and after the victory, he would establish himself as shogun. Prior to the Genpei war, the Hōjō clan was a small family from Izu prefecture, located to the south-east of Tokyo. The leader of this clan was Hōjō Tokimasa, and his daughter Masako was married to the leader of the Minamoto clan. This allegiance helped Minamoto no Yoritomo in the Genpei War and as a reward, Hōjō Tokimasa was given the role of advisor to the new shogun. After Minamoto suddenly passed away in 1199, Hōjō Tokimasa became shikken, regent of the shogunate. This was due to his grandsons being considered too young to rule. This gave the Hōjō family the power of the Kamakura shogunate and essentially made them the rulers of Japan.

Even though the emperor of Japan was alive, he was by this point merely a figurehead. The shikken ruled from Kamakura, a town just south of Tokyo. While in power, the Hōjō clan established a council of state and introduced the country's first military code of law, the Goseibai Shikimoku. The Kamakura shogunate had people in prefectures across the country who would collect taxes as well as shugo, protectors who would oversee each area and keep the peace. And keep the peace they did, as the era of the Kamakura shogunate was a prosperous and relatively peaceful one, although there was resentment towards the Hōjō clan for their dictatorship over the country.

17 members of the Hōjō clan would hold power in Japan for 150 years, until the 14th century when they were overthrown and a new shogunate was established. A series of defences against invading Mongol forces between 1274 and 1281 left the Kamakura shogunate weak in terms of finances and military power. In 1318, Go-Daigo would become emperor, and he wanted to remove the Hōjō clan from power. The Genkō War was fought between 1331 and 1333, ending when the imperial forces, led by Go-Daigo, overthrew the Hōjō clan and established the Kenmu Restoration, restoring imperial rule over Japan.

MAIN Perhaps the most well-known leader of the Hōjō clan was Hōjō Tokimune, the eighth shikken and leader during the Mongol invasions of Japan

TOP RIGHT The Hōjō clan is important in the history of Japan as it expanded Buddhism around the country, especially Zen Buddhism

RIGHT The Hōjō family crest was the Mitsuuroko, or the 'Three Scales' and this symbol can still be seen around Japan today

HŌJŌ CLAN

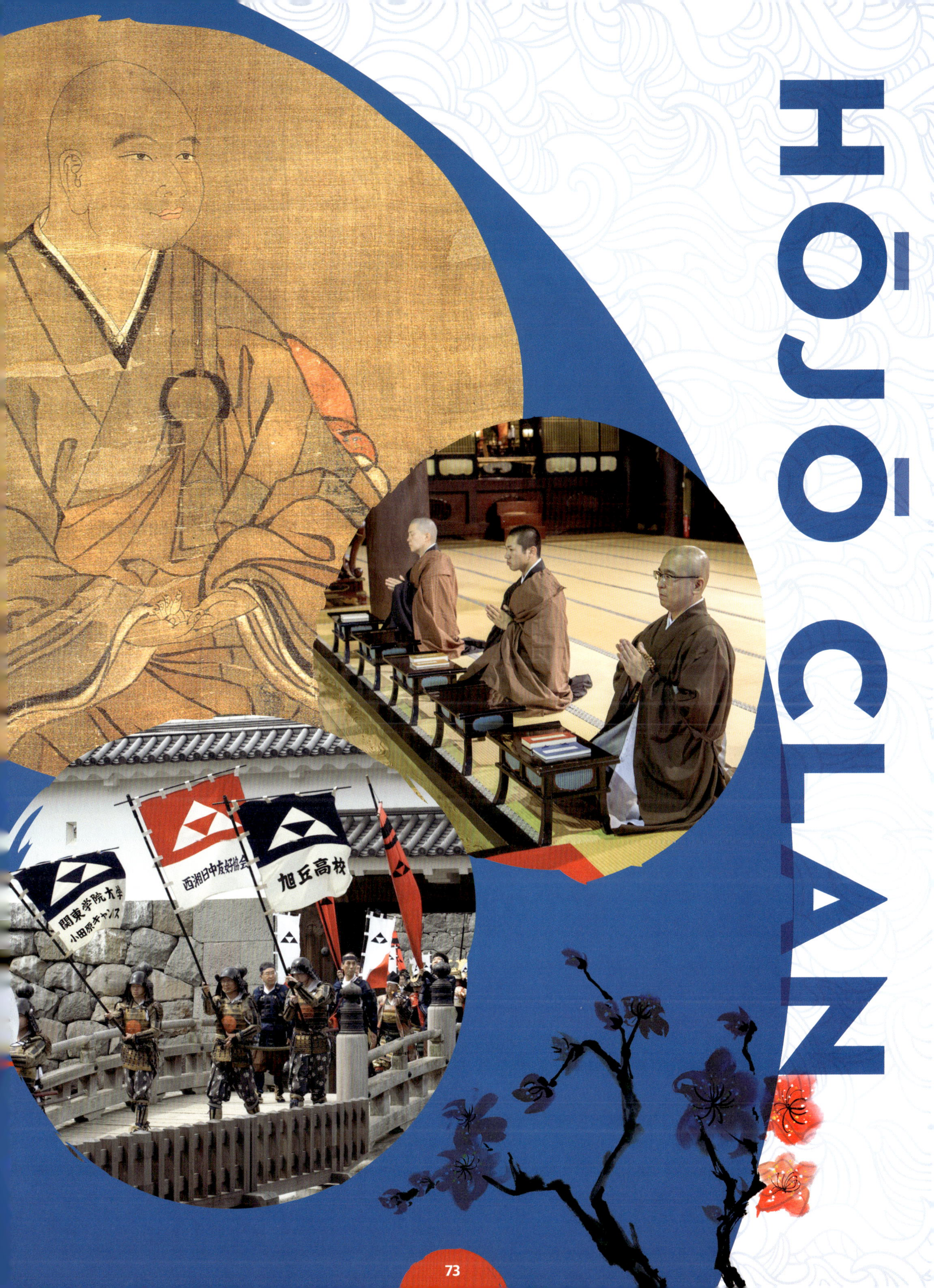

DIVINE WIND
REPELLING THE MONGOL INVASION

THIRSTY FOR CONQUEST DESPITE RULING OVER THE VAST MONGOL EMPIRE, KUBLAI KHAN LONGED TO BRING JAPAN TO HEEL, BUT HIS DREAMS WOULD BE DESTROYED BY THE WRATH OF MOTHER NATURE

By 1268, Kublai Khan, grandson of the great Genghis, was eight years into his reign as the supreme ruler of the vast Mongol Empire, and yet, despite holding the fate of millions of lives and square miles in his hands, he was far from satisfied. For one nation continued to defy him: Japan.

After a reluctant king of Korea (a land the Mongols invaded nine times between 1231 and 1257) failed to deliver envoys dispatched by Kublai, the Mongol warlord took it upon himself to write to the Japanese. With the customary Mongol modesty, he addressed himself as "master of the universe" before imploring the "small state" to engage in friendly relations and then signing off with "nobody would wish to resort to arms".

The letter found its way to the military government in Kamakura, who passed it onto the imperial court in Kyoto. More than a little offended, the administerial government (Japan operated two governments at the time) refused to reply and did what any sensible court would do upon gravely slighting an insatiable khan: they prayed. As for the samurai in Kamakura, they were instructed to prepare for invasion and make their way to the island of Kyushu, the most likely landing place for a Mongol fleet.

Unwilling to accept Japan's intransigence, Kublai ordered the put-upon Korean king to construct an invasion fleet while the great khan continued to send envoys across the sea, many of whom were returned without their heads.

In 1274, Kublai sailed a fleet of 15,000 Yuan and 8,000 Korean troops to the island of Tsushima, where 80 samurai awaited them (the idea that the samurai flocked in countless numbers to defend Japan is somewhat of a myth. Some came, signed a document to prove it, and then promptly left, while others focused more on the rewards gathering a few Mongol heads could secure them. Some never even deigned to answer the call). Needless to say, the 80 fought well but were quickly cut down. As for the local women, holes were punched into their hands, through which a rope was passed, binding them into a literal trail of agony. Others were killed and then strapped to the side of Mongol boats.

Landing at Hakata Bay, the Mongols were confronted by a far larger defence force set on defending Kyushu, which they did, driving the Mongols back. However, it wasn't a typhoon that spared the island but a lack of Mongol supplies combined with a key commander taking an arrow to the face and requiring evacuation. Japan had been saved – for now.

In 1281, after ordering two fleets to be built, Kublai sent another armada to Japan. The Eastern fleet boasted 40,000 men, while the Southern consisted of 100,000. The former reached Japan first,

DIVINE WIND

where it was meant to wait before attacking Hakata Bay alongside the Southern fleet. However, for some reason, its commanders sailed straight into the bay and a ferocious Japanese resistance that now stood behind walls that lined the shore. A storm of arrows and repeated cavalry charges held the Mongols back.

Eventually, the Southern ships arrived - only to be wrecked by a savage typhoon hailed as a 'divine wind' (or kamikaze, a term that would take on a different meaning in later conflicts). As for their Eastern counterparts, many were abandoned when their ships turned for home, leaving the stragglers to be butchered. Never mind the universe, Kublai wasn't even the master of Kyushu. Japan no longer needed to fear invasion.

MAIN This stunning woven silk tapestry depicts the failed Mongol invasion of Japan in 1274

TOP The invasion fleet is splintered by daring samurai raids and ferocious winds in the battle of Hakata Bay, 1281

ABOVE Japanese cavalry bravely charge into the Mongol ranks as they attempt to gain a foothold on the island of Kyushu

NORTH VS SOUTH

THE NANBOKU-CHŌ ERA SAW TWO RIVAL FACTIONS COMPETING FOR IMPERIAL POWER, WHILE IN PRACTICAL TERMS THE ASHIKAGA RULED

For much of the 14th century Japan was embroiled in a civil war of two rival courts; one based in Kyoto and one in nearby Yoshino. The Northern Court were the pretenders to the crown and their rulers are referred to historically as the Northern Court Emperors, to distinguish them from the true rulers at the Southern Court – yet paradoxically it's the Northern Court's descendants who sit on the Chrysanthemum Throne today.

The confusion emerged from a power vacuum. The previously powerful Hōjō clan, who had wielded their shadowy control over the Kamakura shogunate for more than a century, had been wrongfooted by the failed Mongol invasions of Japan. Despite seeing off the enemy, their vassals could not be paid off with grants of new lands, the traditional reward for victory, as Japan had repelled an invasion, not prosecuted a war. The Hōjō attempted to quell resentment by keeping land and titles within their clan, which although showed no favouritism to any others and shored up their immediate grasp of resources and political power, drastically weakened their outside alliances. When a coalition of resentful clans banded together to oust them, the friendless Hōjō were easily toppled.

Into this vacuum stepped Emperor Go-Daigo. He took back practical rule from the Kamakura shogunate, who were reeling from the absence of their Hōjō puppet-masters. But Go-Daigo didn't just want to re-establish the active rule of the emperor; he also wanted to bring back a host of court ceremonies and rules that the shogunate had dismissed. This was his downfall. The new shogun, Ashikaga Takauji, whom Go-Daigo himself had appointed, turned on his imperial sponsor and lent his support instead to the would-be Emperor Kogon, a cousin of Go-Daigo's from another branch of the imperial line: the Northern Court. Takauji's decision precipitated the Nanboku-chō War with ideological battle lines drawn between those who favoured a return to imperial governance and those who believed in a military regime, like the previous Kamakura shogunate. Ironically, although Takauji's defection had been the touchpaper for the conflict, for over a decade he was shogun in name only as even his own clan thought him unfit to rule, with the practicalities of governance undertaken by his brother Tadayoshi. Disagreements between the Ashikaga brothers eventually precipitated the Kanno Incident, in which Tadayoshi had one of his brother's henchmen assassinated and was forced into a Buddhist monastery as punishment. The Southern Court took advantage of the tensions to make another unsuccessful play for their rightful throne. The true victors however were the Ashikaga: they continued to rule for nearly a century after the Southern Court eventually gave up on their quest for the restoration of legitimate imperial power.

MAIN Go-Daigo was the Emperor of the Southern Court faction, finally declared the legitimate imperial line centuries later

RIGHT Kogon was the Northern Court Emperor, a pretender to the throne. Nonetheless Japan's current imperial dynasty are his descendants

FAR RIGHT The first Ashikaga shogun, Takauji, sided with the Northern Court, precipitating an imperial crisis

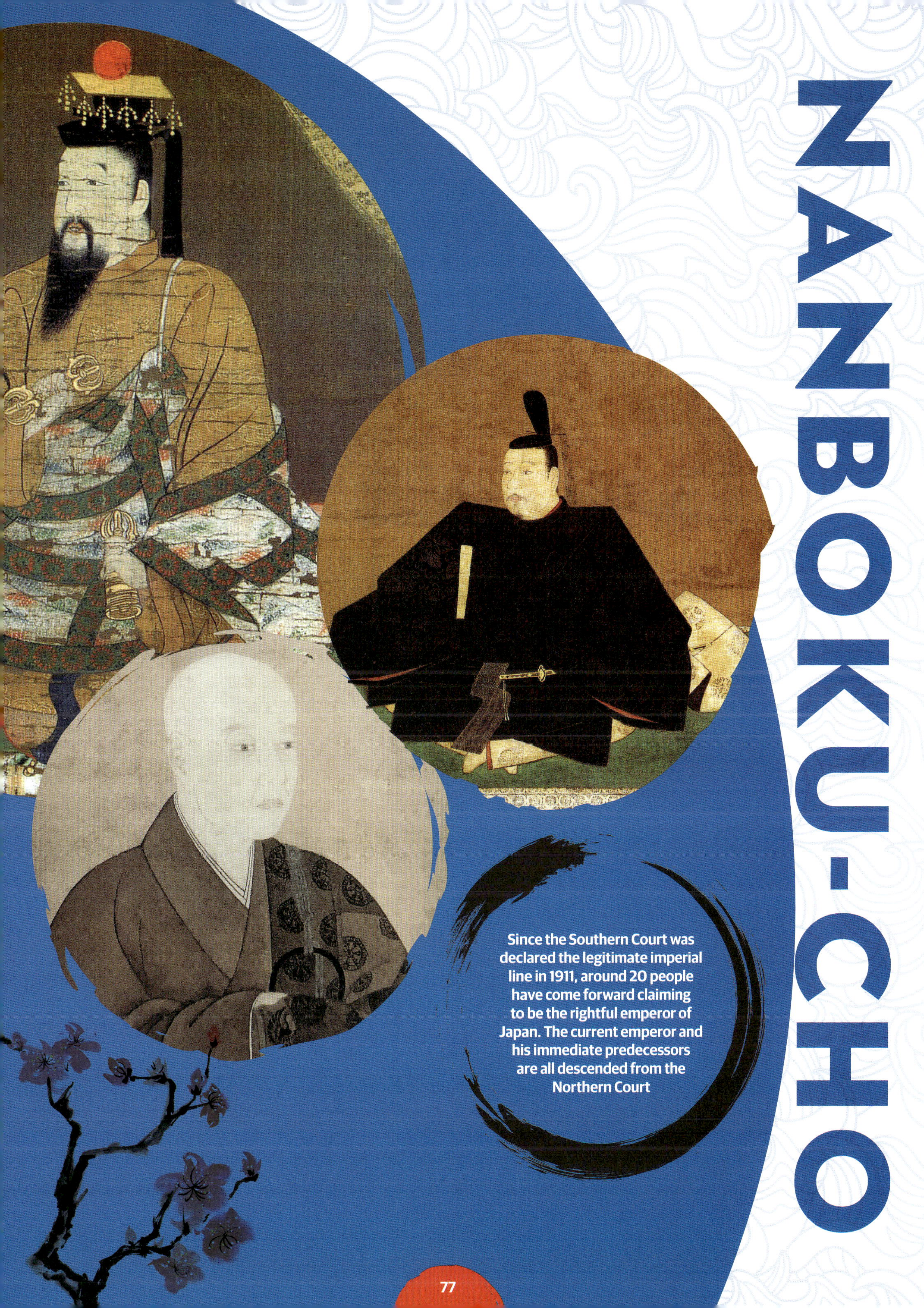

Since the Southern Court was declared the legitimate imperial line in 1911, around 20 people have come forward claiming to be the rightful emperor of Japan. The current emperor and his immediate predecessors are all descended from the Northern Court

THE FAMILY FROM THE FLOWER PALACE

THE ASHIKAGA SHOGUNATE WOULD LITERALLY DIVIDE THE COUNTRY IN TWO, WITH JAPAN BEING SPLIT INTO NORTH AND SOUTH

After Emperor Go-Daigo led a successful uprising against the Hōjō clan he restored power to the imperial family. But this wouldn't last long as Emperor Go-Daigo lost favour with many of the samurai clans that assisted the new emperor. Many of the clans weren't happy with their spoils from helping Emperor Go-Daigo regain power. One of these was Ashikaga Takauji, who warned Go-Daigo that people had expressed they wanted things to go back to how they were in the Heian period.

Ashikaga Takauji established his own shogunate in Kyoto in 1336, shortly after helping Go-Daigo regain power, but there were disputes between the emperor and Takauji over how Japan should be ruled. Go-Daigo ordered forces to kill Takauji and while Takauji's forces lost at the Battle of Takenoshita, Takauji regrouped before bringing his forces to Kyoto to confront the emperor. Ashikaga Takauji successfully fought at the Battle of Minatogawa and marched into Kyoto. Go-Daigo fled the city and Japan was split into two sections, with the Northern Court overseen by the newly formed Ashikaga shogunate, who crowned Prince Yutahito as emperor, as he was loyal to Ashikaga Takauji. Meanwhile, the Southern Court was held by Go-Daigo. The two courts would fight continuously over the following decades, with the two emperors trying to seize total power.

The Ashikaga shogunate ruled from the Flower Palace on Muromachi Street in Kyoto, leading to the clan often being referred to as the Muromachi shogunate, and the era of their power dubbed the Muromachi period.

Yoshimitsu was arguably the most influential shogun of the Ashikaga shogunate. In 1392 he ended the conflict between Northern and Southern courts when he negotiated an outcome that involved alternating succession to the throne, and established peace for a short time. This peace eventually led to the influence of the shogunate being lessened.

Unlike the Kamakura shogunate, the Ashikaga clan gave more power to the samurai and allowed them control over their own land. These rulers would come to be known as daimyo. This would end up coming to hurt the shogunate as the daimyo would fight amongst themselves for more power and this struggle would lead to the Ōnin War.

Despite being a time of conflict in Japan, culturally it was flourishing. Zen Buddhism grew in popularity and, due to trade coming from outside countries, including China, the art scene began to thrive too. This period is also noteworthy because it was at this time that the first traders from Europe arrived in Japan – when Portuguese traders reached the country in 1543. In 1573 the Ashikaga shogunate was ended when Oda Nobunaga seized Kyoto.

MAIN Rather than rule the entire Northern Court alone, the Ashikaga shogunate gave the daimyo power to rule their own lands

RIGHT In 1337 Emperor Go-Daigo fled Kyoto, moving south to the mountains of Yoshino and establishing the Southern Court

FAR RIGHT Ashikaga Takauji would go on to be shogun when he led an uprising against Emperor Go-Daigo, ruling the Northern Court from Kyoto

ASHIKAGA

SENGOKU PERIOD

15TH CENTURY

1467-77

EMPERORS, SHOGUN & DAIMYO 15TH CENTURY

During the late medieval period, the emperor is officially the ruler of Japan but his role is largely ceremonial. Real power lies in the hands of the shogun, a noble warlord who forms a feudal military government. In the 15th century the shogunate gradually loses control over the subordinate daimyo lords who proceed to plunge the country into disorder. Ashikaga Yoshimasa (left, 1436-90) is the ruling shogun at the beginning of the Sengoku period.

ŌNIN WAR 1467-77

A dispute between the Hosokawa and Yamana clans escalates into a nationwide civil war involving the Ashikaga shogunate and several daimyo across Japan. The war turns the Ashikaga shoguns into puppets of the Hosokawa until the 1550s and also initiates the Sengoku period. Right: The magnificent pagoda of Daigo-ji Buddhist temple in Kyoto, built in 951, is one of the few ancient buildings to survive the destruction of the Ōnin War.

BATTLE OF NAGASHINO
28 JUNE 1575

Nobunaga and fellow daimyo Tokugawa Ieyasu lead a large army to relieve Nagashino Castle, which is besieged by Takeda Katsuyori. Using defensive positions, harquebusiers and spearmen, Nobunaga staves off a charge by Katsuyori. His samurai then engage in a fierce melee with the Takeda clansmen. Nobunaga's decisive outcome is hailed as Japan's first 'modern' battle.

03

BATTLE OF OKEHAZAMA
MAY-JUNE 1560

02

2,000-3,000 Oda clansmen led by daimyo Oda Nobunaga dramatically defeat the combined forces of 25,000 warriors from the Imagawa and Matsudaira clans. Using gathered intelligence, Nobunaga wins by launching a surprise attack. A significant turning point in Japanese history, Nobunaga earns the fealty of many samurai and minor warlords.

SIEGE OF SHIGISAN
1577

Forces of Nobunaga take Shigisan Castle from the Matsunaga clan to consolidate power in the Kansai area. The Matsunaga commander, Danjo Hisahide, commits ritual suicide with his son upon his defeat. Before he dies, Hisahide (a master of the tea ceremony) smashes his favourite tea bowl so that it does not fall into the hands of his enemies.

04

1555 — 1560 — 1570 — 1575 — 1577 — 1582 — CONTINUES

01

BATTLE OF MIYAJIMA
16 OCTOBER 1555

The powerful Ōuchi clan is defeated by the numerically inferior forces of daimyo Mōri Motonari on the sacred island of Miyajima in Aki Province. The Mori clan are subsequently able to establish a foremost position in western Japan. Below: The forces of Motonari arrive by ship to Miyajima.

ISHIYAMA HONGAN-JI WAR
AUGUST 1570 - AUGUST 1580

Oda Nobunaga's forces fight a ten-year war against a powerful faction of religious zealots called the Ikko-ikki. The Ikko-ikki's's central base is the cathedral fortress of Ishiyama Hongan-ji. Nobunaga and his allies attack Ikki communities and fortifications in nearby provinces to weaken their support structure. Much of the fighting occurs at three sieges of Nagashima while Ishiyama Hongan-ji surrenders to Nobunaga. The fortress wall of Osaka Castle is built on the former site of the Ishiyama Hongan-ji Temple.

05

BATTLE OF YAMAZAKI
2 JULY 1582

Akechi Mitsuhide, a retainer of Nobunaga, forces his master to commit ritual suicide and then assumes power. Nobunaga's subordinate, Toyotomi Hideyoshi, marches to confront Mitsuhide and engages him in a fierce battle. Hideyoshi wins the battle while Mitsuhide flees and is killed by bandits in the aftermath.

MAJOR ENGAGEMENTS

"HIDEYOSHI INTENDS TO CONQUER MING CHINA AND PLANS TO INVADE THROUGH KOREA. WHEN THE KOREANS REFUSE TO GRANT PASSAGE, HIDEYOSHI MAKES KOREA THE FIRST STAGE OF CONQUEST"

1583

1590

06

BATTLE OF SHIZUGATAKE

10-11 JUNE 1583

Hideyoshi is now the most powerful man in Japan but a line of his fortresses (including Shizugatake) above Lake Biwa are attacked by opposing Oda forces. Hideyoshi swiftly advances on Shizugatake and the Oda are defeated after being forced to adopt a hasty defensive posture. Hirano Nagayasu is one of the 'Seven Spears of Shizugatake' who are mounted bodyguards for Hideyoshi. They successfully charge at a decisive moment of the battle and earn much fame and honour.

07

SIEGE OF ODAWARA

MAY - AUGUST 1590

Hideyoshi aims to eliminate the threat of the Hōjō clan to his power. The Hōjō hastily improve the defences of Odawara Castle before Hideyoshi's forces besiege it. The siege sees very little action with the besiegers enjoying entertainments while the defenders sleep on the ramparts. The castle surrenders after three months of siege. Odawara is later reconstructed into its present form by one of Tokugawa Iesayu's retainers. It is now designated as a National Historic Monument.

09

BATTLE OF SEKIGAHARA

21 OCTOBER 1600

Hideyoshi's death leads to a power struggle between Tokugawa Ieyasu and an alliance led by Ishida Mitsunari. At Sekigahara, Mitsunari is betrayed during the battle by his ally Kobayakawa Hideaki. Mitsunari is killed and Iesayu's victory eventually leads to the Tokugawa shogunate, which is the last to control Japan until 1868.

BATTLE OF TENNOJI

3 JUNE 1615

The Siege of Osaka climaxes with a battle outside the castle. Hideyori plans to lead the garrison against Iesayu's numerically superior force with other attacks elsewhere from his allies Akashi Morishige and Sanada Yukimura. The battle goes awry when Yukimara is killed and Morishige's encircling force is intercepted. When Iesayu's men enter the castle, Hideyori commits suicide in the keep. The last resistance to the Tokugawa shogunate is eliminated.

1592 — 1600 — 1614 — 1615

08

JAPANESE INVASIONS OF KOREA

23 MAY 1592 - 16 DECEMBER 1598

Hideyoshi intends to conquer Ming China and plans to invade through Korea. When the Koreans refuse to grant passage, Hideyoshi makes Korea the first stage of conquest. Two invasions are launched in the samurai's only assault on a foreign country. The Japanese even reach Manchuria but the Koreans and Chinese vigorously fight back. After Hideyoshi's death, Japanese armies withdraw from Korea.

Left: Japanese forces perform an amphibious landing before besieging the fortress at Busan, Korea.

10

SIEGE OF OSAKA

8 NOVEMBER 1614 - 22 JANUARY 1615, MAY - JUNE 1615

The Tokugawa shogunate is contested by a daimyo alliance led by Hideyoshi's son Toyotomi Hideyori. His followers gather at Osaka Castle, which is then besieged by Ieyasu. After a winter bombardment a peace treaty is organised but Hideyori soon declares Ieyasu to be a rebel to the imperial throne and the siege resumes.

THE SHADOW WARRIORS

THE SHINOBI WERE TRAINED TO BE MASTERS OF FIGHTING, ESPIONAGE AND SABOTAGE. WHILE THEY WERE NOT HONOURABLE, THEY WERE ESSENTIAL IN WAR

Ninjas, or as they were actually known in Japan, 'shinobi', were masters of deception, infiltration, sabotage and fighting. Often hired by samurai, their goal typically was to spy on enemies by travelling into hostile environments and collecting information. They were also known for sabotaging enemy fortresses, most commonly by starting fires. The samurai would not do these acts themselves as they were not a part of 'Bushido', the samurai's moral code.

The first reference to shinobi comes from the 8th century, but the first record of these warriors being trained and employed wasn't until the Sengoku period in the 15th century. This time was tumultuous and it created demand for people willing to commit these acts.

Like the samurai, shinobi were born into the profession and taught by masters of the craft. From a young age, they would be trained in the arts of stealth, spying and survival. Today this would be known as 'ninjutsu', but there is no evidence that this term was used at the time. A lot of the teachings of shinobi were derived from the 13th chapter of Sun Tzu's Art of War, which explained methods of espionage.

There are a number of misconceptions about shinobi. For example, while assassinations were conducted by these warriors, this was incredibly rare and there are few historical examples of this. Shinobi were used more often to spy on or sabotage enemies. Another common misconception about ninjas is the clothes they would wear.

They are typically depicted in all-black outfits; Hollywood movies such as the James Bond film You Only Live Twice fuelled this idea. Yet, there is no historical evidence of these clothes being worn. Ninjas would typically be dressed as regular citizens to avoid drawing attention to themselves. Common disguises included merchants, monks, entertainers and samurai, as they would wear baggy clothing, perfect for concealing weapons. Sometimes, shinobi are depicted wearing black in art as it emphasised their stealthiness, but no records show them actually wearing all-black.

Shinobi used a plethora of tools depending on what their mission was. Ropes and grappling hooks were common for infiltration as well as chisels, hammers and picks to help create holes in walls to use as footholds. The kunai, a pointed tool, was also used for this purpose, although it is typically depicted in modern media as a weapon. The katana was the weapon of choice as its length was also helpful for prodding. The kusarigama was a sickle with a weighted chain and it had multiple uses, as the blade could cut ropes, while the weighted chain could be thrown at enemy weapons and then pulled to disarm opponents.

MAIN The stereotypical black clothing of the ninjas comes from theatre where actors used the black outfits to hide their presence

RIGHT Ninjas would typically wear normal baggy clothes that could be used to hide any weapons as well as not raise suspicion

FAR RIGHT A kusarigama. The weight on the end of the chain would be whipped at enemies to disarm their weapon

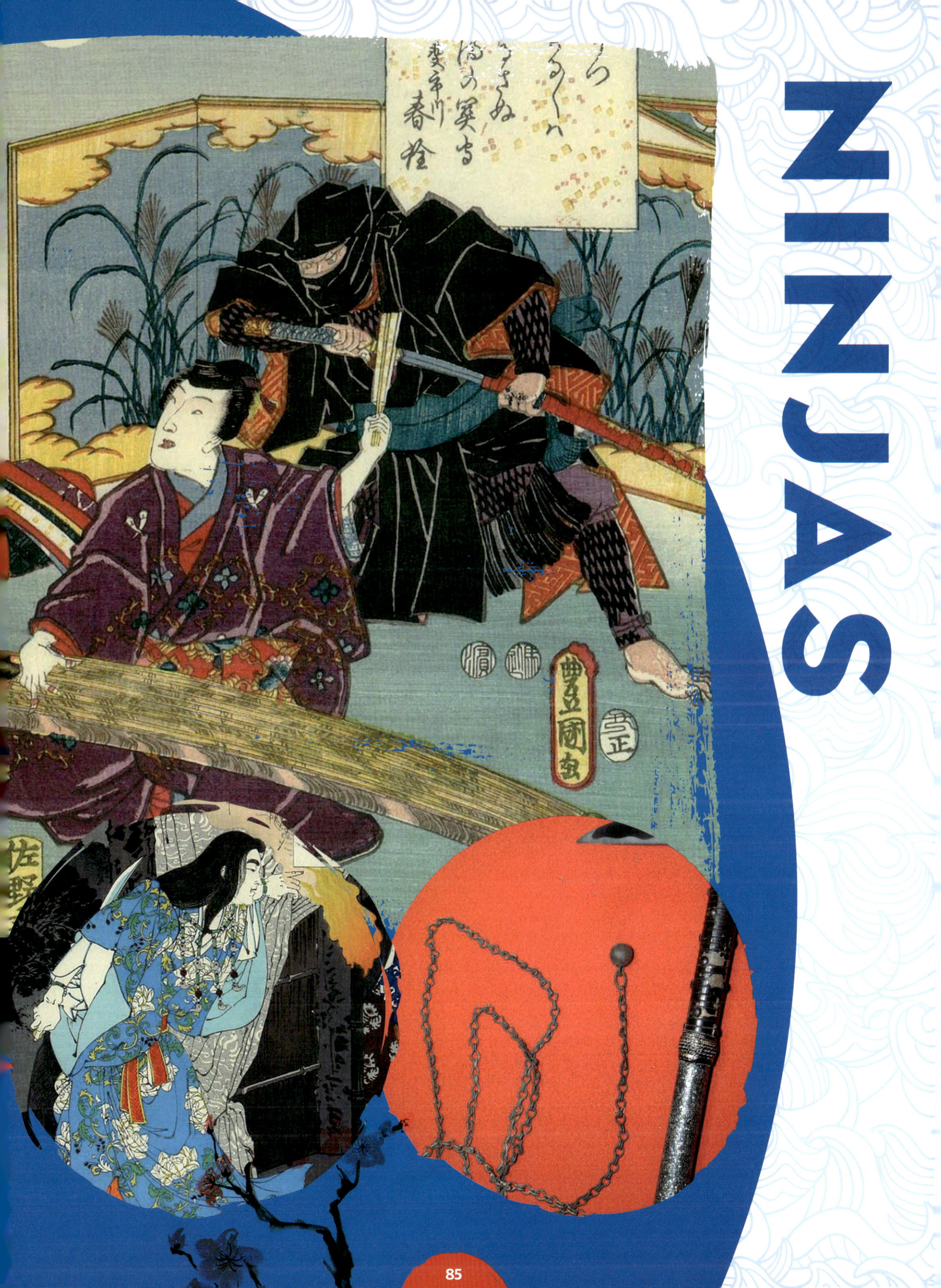
NINJAS

THE NANBAN TRADE ERA

THE FIRST EUROPEANS TO VISIT JAPAN BROUGHT FIREARMS, FABRICS AND NEW TECHNOLOGY – BUT ALSO A THREAT TO THE JAPANESE ORDER

The Portuguese had been trading with China since around 1514 and, at this time, there was a trade embargo between China and Japan. The Portuguese traders saw this as an opportunity to act as a mediator between the two countries and made their first contact with Japan in 1542, arriving the following year to begin trading. The Dutch would soon follow in 1600. These new visitors were impressed by Japan's precious metals, such as silver, and by the craftsmanship of Japan's swords. The word 'nanban' was used in Japan originally to refer to people from other South Asian countries, but after the Portuguese arrived the word took on a new meaning, referring to people from the West.

The trade from Europe brought firearms to Japan and the Portuguese were happy to exchange these weapons as long as Japan welcomed Jesuit missionaries into the country, bringing Christianity to Japan. At the time, Japan was full of warring factions who were more than willing to welcome these people if it meant they had weapons that gave them an advantage in battle.

The Europeans also brought fabrics, such as silk from China, and the Japanese were more than willing to trade with the Dutch and Portuguese rather than trading with their Chinese enemies for it! Trade also brought new shipbuilding techniques to Japan, leading to the construction of the Red-Seal Ships (shuinsen). Using elements of the European galleon, these trade ships would reach out to other countries for further trade routes.

Ōmura Sumitada was the first daimyo to allow foreign trade in, through a port in Nagasaki. He was also the first lord to convert to Christianity. Shortly after converting he ordered the destruction of Shinto shrines as well as Buddhist temples. By 1580 there were roughly 150,000 Christians in Japan.

As the number of Christians began to grow in Japan, it began to be seen as a threat to the country's culture and traditions. Toyotomi Hideyoshi in 1587 ordered all Christian priests to leave Japan but

MAIN Artist's depiction of Portuguese traders arriving in Nagasaki. It shows Jesuit missionaries arriving in Japan and offering goods from their boat

ABOVE RIGHT Portuguese traders were enamoured by the craftsmanship the Japanese could produce. This item was commissioned by the Society of Jesus in the 16th century

TOP RIGHT A Red-Seal Ship. These vessels were inspired by the european galleon-style boats that made their way to Japan

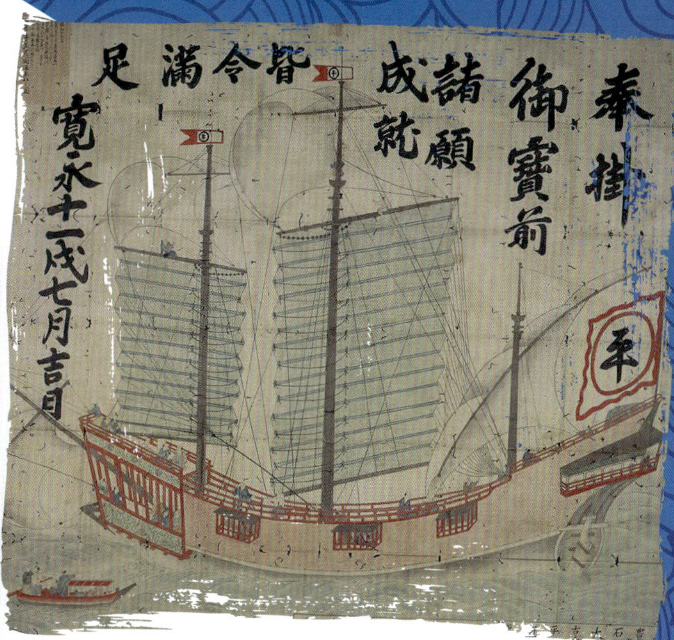

in 1593, Dominican and Augustinian friars arrived and began openly preaching in Japan. When Tokugawa Ieyasu took power following Toyotomi Hideyoshi's death, he restricted all trade with Christians to Nagasaki, so it was easy to monitor them. In 1614 the Jesuits were expelled from Japan and the country would slowly close its doors to all outsiders. Any foreigners arriving in Japan would face persecution or the death penalty. Firearms were made illegal and so was the building of large ships and travelling abroad. Japan completely cut itself off from the rest of the world and would remain isolated for over 250 years with the exception of a few strictly monitored Dutch traders accepted in Nagasaki.

DAIMYO
THE WARLORDS OF JAPAN

IN THE BLOODSOAKED CHAOS OF NATIONWIDE CIVIL WAR, THE DAIMYO, THE POWERFUL SAMURAI LORDS OF JAPAN, BATTLED FOR SUPREMACY

Japan has a long history of feudal warfare. Such conflict reached its apogee during the Sengoku Jidai, 'the Age of the Country at War', that stretched from 1467 until 1615. The warlords of this fractured Japan, riven by civil wars, were known as daimyo, the 'Great Names', that ruled over large territories of the country.

The daimyo proper, as opposed to the traditional aristocrats of medieval Japan, traced their origin to the heyday of the Ashikaga shoguns. The 14th century witnessed the rise of a new samurai aristocracy known as the shugo. Originally, military governors serving the prior Kamakura bakufu (military government) and they were subsequently integral members of the following Ashikaga shogunate. Like the daimyo, the shugo were the lords of their own domains.

ABOVE Victory at the 1600 Battle of Sekigahara paved the way for the Sengoku Jidai daimyo Tokugawa Ieyasu to become the overlord of all Japan

The power of the Ashikaga Shogunate declined precipitously in the late 15th century. The country had been shaken by a series of devastating peasant revolts. Then the ten-year Ōnin War (1467-77) between two rival clans, the Hosokawa and the Yamana, was fought over the control of Kyoto, Japan's capital, and the seat of the emperor himself. Much of the old city of Kyoto was destroyed in the conflict, and the authority of the Ashikaga was largely ruined along with it.

HŌJŌ SŌUN: THE FIRST DAIMYO

The disruption of traditional lines of authority that followed the Ōnin War opened up opportunities for ruthless samurai to grab a share of power using any means they possibly could. Old families of ancient lineage could be knocked from their perches by aggressive underlings, or perhaps they could even be annihilated altogether.

This era of instability and civil war that engulfed Japan, the Sengoku Jidai, allowed for the true daimyo to come to the fore. The subversion of lordly aristocrats by persons substantially lower on the social scale was termed gekokujō, 'the low overcoming the high.'

Thus, the prototypical daimyo, Hōjō Sōun (1432-1519), had himself initially been only an ordinary samurai. He put down a rebel leader in Ise province in 1491 and for his good work was put in charge of the region. He and his sons relentlessly enlarged their holdings in ensuing years. In addition to being an excellent soldier, Sōun, who would live until the ripe old age of 88, showed a flair for good governance. The law code he promulgated would provide a legal template for other daimyo.

THE RIVALS: TAKEDA SHINGEN & UESUGI KENSHIN

The Sengoku Jidai would see the rise of several legendary daimyo. Among the foremost of these warlords were the great rivals Takeda Shingen and Uesugi Kenshin. Takeda Shingen (1521-73) was the master of Kai province in modern-day Yamanashi prefecture, while Uesugi Kenshin (1530-78) ruled Echigo province in north-central Japan. Both were, in addition to being daimyo, Buddhist monks. Each had shown ruthlessness in achieving power in their respective domains. Shingen had mounted a coup against his own father, a daimyo who had planned to pass over him and give his lands to another, younger son.

An excellent general, Shingen was also known as a wise and generous civil administrator. The peasant farmers of Kai were relatively well treated in comparison to those ruled by other daimyo, and they gave Shingen their loyalty.

Kenshin's ascent was even more dramatic. Originally named Nagao Kagetora, he was a vassal of the more powerful Uesugi clan. However, the Uesugi fell on hard times during the Sengoku Jidai, and this opened the door for Kenshin to step through. After a series of defeats had left the Uesugi clan prostrate, its chief, Uesugi Norimasa, appealed to his vassal for succour.

This was granted, but Kagetora did so on the condition that he be adopted as the Uesugi heir and also be made the lord of Echigo. He changed his name to Uesugi Kenshin.

Shinano province lay between the domains of Uesugi Kenshin and

Takeda Shingen, and it became their battleground. They would meet in five separate battles at Kawanakajima, a strategically important piece of land, between 1553 and 1564. These were fought with large doses of chivalry. The greatest and most dramatic of the encounters, the fourth battle, was fought in 1561. When news reached Uesugi that Takeda's salt supply had been disrupted by another daimyo, he delivered some of his own to his enemy, saying that he battled with a sword, not salt.

ODA NOBUNAGA

After the unraveling of the Ashikaga shogunate following the Ōnin War, Japan would be bereft of a central government for over a century. The civil wars would come to an end only with the appearance of three remarkable daimyo. The first of these was Oda Nobunaga.

THE 47 RŌNIN

In 1701, a lesser daimyo of Harima province, Asano Naganori, was goaded into wounding Lord Kira Yoshinaka, an obnoxious government official of the Tokugawa Shogunate. Merely unsheathing his blade in the shogun's palace in Edo was a grave crime carrying a penalty of death. Even though he had been provoked by Kira's insults, Asano's offence could not be excused. He was made to take his own life by committing seppuku, ritual suicide, and his territory was seized.

The death of Asano left his former samurai without a master. They had become rōnin, and 47 of them would not allow his death to pass unavenged. They devised a plan to strike back at Kira. To prevent him from learning of their intent, they went their separate ways, pretended to have dispensed with being samurai, and had no contact with one another.

Then one snowy December evening in 1702, the 47 rōnin mounted a surprise attack on Kira's townhouse inside Edo. Kira's own samurai fought the rōnin hard in defence of their lord, but at last, Kira was captured. The leader of the 47, Ōishi Yoshio, beheaded him with the very dagger that Asano had used to commit seppuku. Kira's head was carried to Asano's tomb in the city and placed on it.

The plan had succeeded, but the 46 surviving rōnin could not be allowed to get away with murder, no matter how much their actions may have accorded with the ideal of samurai loyalty. Each man was himself made to commit suicide, and join their lord in death.

ABOVE The 47 rōnin went to extraordinary lengths to obtain vengeance for their dead master, the ill-fated Lord Asano

The son of an unimportant daimyo in Owari province, Oda won a surprising victory over a much stronger opponent in 1560 at the Battle of Okehazama. In 1568, he was in control of Kyoto, and the shogun, Ashikaga Yoshiaki, was his own creature. In 1573, Yoshiaki made the mistake of going against Oda, who drove him into exile. A good portion of Kyoto was burned in the process. The Ashikaga Shogunate, for so long toothless, was now truly finished.

Oda was an enthusiastic adopter of firearms, the first of which had been brought to Japan by Portuguese traders. His arquebusiers, deployed in lines and firing in disciplined volleys, decimated the charging cavalry of the Takeda clan (the formidable Takeda Shingen was now dead) at the Battle of Nagashino in 1575.

Oda's control over Japan increased over the next few years, and he would eventually corral 22 provinces into submission. However, in 1582 he would be betrayed by one of his own vassals while in Kyoto's Honnō-ji temple. The building itself was aflame, and like a true samurai, Oda committed seppuku (ritual suicide) rather than live with the indignity of defeat.

TOYOTOMI HIDEYOSHI

One of Oda's subordinates, Toyotomi Hideyoshi, seized the chance brought into being by Oda's slaying to take vengeance on the perpetrators. An extremely capable general of low birth, Hideyoshi vaulted to the pinnacle of power, and he set about bringing Japan's daimyo under his own domination.

ABOVE One of the greatest of Japan's Sengoku era warlords, in 1582 Oda Nobunaga committed ritual suicide as the Honnoji temple in Kyoto burned around him

With an army of a quarter-million soldiers, he extended his power over the southern Japanese islands of Kyushu and Shikoku in 1587. By 1590, he had secured the submission of the last remaining independent daimyo in Honshu, Japan's main island. The country had at last been unified. All daimyo swore loyalty oaths to Hideyoshi, getting in return acknowledgments of their rights to their own fiefs.

TOKUGAWA IEYASU

Hideyoshi's 1592 invasion of Korea would last several years and prove to be a bloody, costly failure. His death in 1598 created a path to paramount power for the greatest of the Sengoku daimyo to arise. Tokugawa Ieyasu, a leading vassal of Hideyoshi, had his base at Edo (the future Tokyo). He first defeated a powerful alliance of his enemies at the Battle of Sekigahara in 1600. The last embers of rebellion were finally stamped out with Tokugawa's capture of Osaka Castle in 1615.

These military successes made Tokugawa the unchallenged master of all Japan. Having taken the moribund title of shogun in 1603, he made Edo the seat of the national government. For him, and his descendants who would become shoguns after him, the goal was a stable, peaceful Japan. The land would still be ruled by daimyo, with each man the lord of his domain, but all would acknowledge the Tokugawa shogun as his supreme overlord.

RŌNIN: MEN OF THE WAVES

The samurai, so strongly linked to his daimyo, might well find himself without a lord, depending upon the fortunes of war or other vicissitudes of life. These samurai without masters were known as rōnin, 'men of the waves'. Though they may have lacked masters, they still possessed their superlative military skills, and they were a ready source of recruits for a daimyo who wished to quickly bulk up his army.

One daimyo, for example, named Kuroda Yoshitaka, shrewdly advised his officials to overlook it if the coins paid to the rōnin were too heavy or if the rōnin pilfered some of them. He needed to bring rōnin to his banner, and having a reputation for generosity was the surest way to do this.

At the end of the Sengoku Jidai, many rōnin made their way to Osaka Castle to defend it against Tokugawa Ieyasu. Such service brought them money, always welcome, and also gave them the chance to take vengeance on the enemy. In the end, Osaka Castle was doomed, and the rōnin inside along with it. After it fell in 1615, many were beheaded by the victorious Tokugawa.

Rōnin might come into existence even after the end of the Age of the Country at War. In the late 19th century, when the forces of the resurgent emperor moved to supplant the Tokugawa shogunate as the central government, they sought the support of the peasantry. To this end, rōnin were used to disseminate the news that taxes would be slashed in half if the imperial side gained power, and the message did not fail to gain adherents for the imperial party.

The memory of the rōnin persists among modern Japanese. The story of the 47 rōnin who took vengeance for their master is justly famous, and even their title is still used. High-school graduates who fail to secure admission to the universities of their choice, and choose to wait a year to take the entrance examinations again, are called rōnin.

ABOVE The Takeda clan horsemen were cut down by Oda Nobunaga's arquebusiers at the Battle of Nagashino

RIGHT Arguably the first of the true daimyo, Hōjō Sōun exemplified the Samurai who had risen from obscurity to a position of power in Japan's unsettled Age of the Country at War

東照神君
伊井直正
木村重成首

ISOLATION NATION

THE TOKUGAWA SHOGUNS REIGNED OVER AN EMPIRE CLOSED TO THE OUTSIDE WORLD – UNTIL THEY WERE FORCED TO PRISE IT OPEN

Shadow emerged from the flames, swaddled in robes that concealed both his weaponry and considerable girth. The victorious warrior Tokugawa Ieyasu quietly took a seat on the soft tatami mats in Kyoto's Imperial Palace. Emperor Go-Yōzei sat one step above him, as was the natural order of things in those days, but make no mistake - Ieyasu held all the power. He had come to ask the emperor a question he couldn't refuse. He wanted to be shogun.

He was the only man in Honshu who could make such an audacious claim. Ieyasu, a military mastermind born to a daimyo (feudal lord) family, had triumphed over the ruling Toyotomi clan at the Battle of Sekigahara in 1600. The usurper then spent the first three years of the 17th century unifying Japan and establishing dominance over other regional powerholders, either killing off disloyal daimyo or placating them with large tracts of land. By the time he got to the emperor in 1603, he was the most powerful man in Japan.

Seal of approval from the emperor received, the new shogun holed himself up in Edo Castle, a heavily fortified and moated complex at the heart of what would become Tokyo. From this new capital city, Ieyasu drew up his plans for a new governmental system (bakufu) that would ensure he wouldn't lose his power as quickly as he had gained it. The 270 remaining daimyo were reorganised along Tokugawa terms. Loyal daimyo (fudai) were placed in strategic positions near Edo, Kyoto and Osaka, whereas troublemakers (tozama) were relegated to Japan's outermost provinces.

A CLASS OF ITS OWN

Ieyasu didn't stop at reshuffling the government - he turned his attention next to the rest of society. If Japan's class system limited upwards mobility before, Ieyasu made it literally illegal. Below the emperor and his court was the shogun, followed by the daimyo, then the samurai. This was the way of things.

All samurai were bound to their local daimyo, just as all the daimyo were bound to the shogun. In return for their submission, the samurai

LEFT Ieyasu examines the head of a fallen enemy after the Battle of Osaka, 1614

were paid a stipend, based on rice farming harvests. If they wished to defect from their daimyo overlords, a samurai would have to give up his weapons and join the peasantry, who comprised about 80 per cent of the population.

Few did, because life for an Edo-era peasant was difficult. The burden of the samurai stipends took up to half of their crop, and there was no chance of making a better life as peasants couldn't engage in anything other than agriculture, or even travel far outside their province. The one upside to being a peasant was the respect it afforded, as Japan's wealth and prosperity came mostly from rice farming. Sadly, this respect for the humble farming man was usually only theoretical.

Beneath the peasantry were the artisans, then the detested merchants, who were held in great suspicion for their profiteering and confined to live in specific urban districts. Below them, the 'untouchables' - people that violated Buddhist principles, such as animal slaughterers, executioners and prostitutes. Ironically, their services were often in heavy demand.

CLOSING THE DOOR

In 1605, just two years after being made shogun, Ieyasu abdicated in favour of his son Hidetada, establishing the Tokugawa dynasty. But never a man to desire retirement, Ieyasu continued to operate as the power behind the throne until his death in 1616.

ABOVE A 17th-century portrait of Tokugawa Ieyasu, the founder and first shogun of Japan's Tokugawa shogunate

For the first time, Japan was not at war with itself, and could focus on the outside world for a change. European traders from Portugal, Spain and the Netherlands had landed on Nippon's shores a century prior, and the unusual goods they brought with them - from eyeglasses to guns - were a hit. Ieyasu saw the benefits of working with these outsiders, not only allowing them to establish trading posts in Japan, but also to settle in the country, if they chose. He personally exchanged gifts with King James I of England (including a new-fangled telescope), keen to establish diplomatic relations with this rich new ally on the other side of the world.

The downside of these foreigners was that they brought an alien religion with them, one that was fast gaining followers, particularly in the area around the port of Nagasaki. For other East Asian nations, Christian missionaries opened the floodgate to full-scale colonisation. Even mighty China had seen Macao siphoned off by the Portuguese. Tokugawa Ieyasu's successors were determined that this should never, ever happen to the country they had fought so hard to win. Why should such a proud, ancient culture need imports from abroad, anyway?

To nip colonialism in the bud, Ieyasu's grandson Tokugawa Iemitsu issued three 'sakoku' ('closed country') edicts in the 1630s that would change Japanese culture, history and even language forever. In 1633, travelling abroad was officially banned for all Japanese citizens. In 1635, Japanese citizens abroad were forbidden to return, on pain of death, and all foreign shipping was restricted to the artificial island of Dejima in Nagasaki. The final edict in 1639 expelled foreigners altogether, except the few Dutch and Chinese traders permitted to stay on Dejima. Japan was officially closed for business.

Western ideas were cast off, and Buddhism, Shintoism and neo-Confucianism became the philosophies of the state. Even receiving a letter from abroad could get you and your whole family killed, such was the fear that Western perspectives could infiltrate Japan and lead to colonialism. An emphasis was placed instead on the traditional Japanese way of life.

With no internal or external enemies to combat, the samurai gradually fell into bureaucratic jobs, while the daimyo raked in taxes as bountiful agricultural production created surpluses. The wily, comfortable merchants, once hated, grew wealthy as a result of political stability and the growing domestic economy. They created their own urban culture, free to pursue leisure and pleasure, while the samurai were discouraged from enjoying such frivolities, bound as they were by their strict moral code called bushidō.

From 1688 to 1704, the Genroku period saw the traditional Japanese arts explode, free to develop entirely without the influence of other cultures. Kabuki dance theatre kept the urbanites enthralled with its dramatic movements, while they marvelled at bunraku puppet performances.

Poignant haiku poetry grew out of an earlier form of satirical prose, haikai, which made listeners laugh until their bellies ached.

STRUGGLING SAMURAI

Sakoku and the prosperity of the commercial classes may have enriched Japan culturally, but it fundamentally altered the traditional rice-based economy. Without new technology from abroad, and a lack of class mobility at home to encourage innovation, agriculture stagnated throughout the 18th century. The samurai and daimyo, who relied upon good rice harvests for their income, fell on hard times. Many took out loans from wealthy merchants and businessmen to stay afloat, a source of great shame for this noble class. Financial troubles shot through the shogunate. Coupled with famine and increasingly higher taxes to prop up the government, the peasants decided that enough was enough. 20 famines between 1675 and 1837 meant the bakufu spent a lot of energy quelling rural uprisings.

But there was another problem brewing on the horizon. A Danish sailor called Shpanberg, acting on behalf of Russia, landed in Kamogawa, Chiba, in 1739. The incident showed that the outside world would soon come knocking. By the time of Matthew Perry's arrival in 1853, the Tokugawa shogunate was so brittle and worn down by infighting and a lack of resources that it wasn't in a position to challenge thinly veiled American threats. So, with the signing of the "unequal treaty" (otherwise known as the Harris Treaty), sakoku came to an end.

Enter the bakumatsu, or 'end of the bakufu'. Disaffected, anti-foreign and influential daimyo in the southwestern domains of Satsuma and Chōshū joined up with conservative samurai to deliver the killer blow to the shogunate and restore the emperor to his traditional position on the Chrysanthemum Throne.

ABOVE Castles played a key role in the bakufu. To limit the power of samurai and daimyo, only one castle was permitted per region

When political manoeuvres failed to prevent the signing of the humiliating Harris Treaty, the so-called "Satchō alliance" armed themselves with the powerful newly available Western weaponry, and overwhelmed the last Tokugawa shogun (with considerably less manpower) in 1866. A couple of years later, the emperor was handed back control of Japan once again, ushering in the Meiji Restoration.

A lengthy 250 years of Tokugawa rule had brought about unprecedented peace, and it had allowed a unique culture to flourish within the bubble it created for itself. But the shogunate was, in many ways, a victim of its own success. Despite the best efforts of Tokugawa traditionalists, the capitalist economy that naturally grew out of political stability overtook agricultural cultivation - without Western help.

Inflexibility imposed by the early shoguns meant that society was unable to change with the times, and without a purpose, the samurai lost the pride that had long sustained them. Ieyasu could hardly have imagined that destroying Japan's age-old power dynamic to place himself at the top would ultimately pave the way for his dynasty's disappointing decline.

CHRISTIANITY GOES UNDERGROUND

The head of a teenage samurai who dared disobey the Tokugawa is spiked onto a pole outside Nagasaki, and thrust into the ground, as a warning to anyone who might think to challenge the shogun. You have been warned - practice Christianity, and you'll be martyred.

Amakusa Shirō was a 17-year-old noble born to Roman Catholic parents. His forefathers and mothers had converted to Christianity after hearing the preaching of Portuguese missionaries, but after Christianity was officially banned by the shogunate in 1613, it became increasingly difficult to practice Christian traditions. So, the charismatic Christian teen led an impromptu army of peasants and masterless samurai (rōnin) in the 1637-38 Shimabara Rebellion, taking over Hara Castle. After five long months, the insurrection was defeated, Shirō executed, and 300,000 Japanese Christians were subjected to religious persecution.

Suspected Christians were tested with blasphemous rituals, such as the fumi-e, where a person was made to step on the image of the face of Christ. They were also required to register at their local Buddhist temple. But punitive measures didn't stop them from devoutly practicing their faith. Instead, Christianity simply went underground, with prayers taking place in secret rooms in the house, and Christian icons swapped out for Buddhist ones. Sakoku meant that Japanese Christians had no contact with other Christians, so 'kakure kirishitans' (as hidden Christians are now known) developed their own distinctive take on this imported religion.

In 2018, the Hidden Christian Sites in the Nagasaki Region were finally recognised by UNESCO as a World Heritage Site.

ABOVE RIGHT Buddhist goddesses such as Guanyin (Avalokiteśvara) were frequently used by kakure kirishitans to covertly represent the Virgin Mary

THE FLOATING WORLD

THE EDO, OR TOKUGAWA PERIOD, WAS AN ERA OF PROSPERITY AND PEACE THAT SAW ART AND CULTURE FLOURISH

Deriving its name from the colloquial 'Oedo', Edo, which we now know as Tokyo ('capital of the East') has been characterised throughout history not just by its highly rigid social structure and enormous economic growth but also for its people's love of culture and the arts.

Between 1603 and 1868 fifteen generations of Tokugawa shogun ruled Japan from the city, relying on a hierarchy that adhered to strict individual, social and economic constraints. The samurai were deemed the most important members of society, followed by farmers and craftsmen. Merchants found themselves on the bottom rung, while many groups avoided classification altogether, notably the Buddhist monks, nobility, Shinto priests, prostitutes and beggars.

As this once small village grew it began to transform into a metropolis. Artisans, merchants and farmers alike gravitated to the city, realising its potential for business. Vendors lined the sides of the roads selling tea, books, overseas fabrics and food. Due to the growing affluence, many Japanese were able to go from only eating two meals per day to enjoying three. Tofu, rice, fish and dried eel were traditional fare, and sushi, which was originally a staple of the working man due to its nutritional content and the fact that it was cheap and easy to prepare, became popular.

In terms of art, the Edo period marked one of the richest periods in Japanese history. The period witnessed a time of relative peace in Japan and, with no wars to fight, the daimyo, shoguns and samurai had to find other pursuits with which to fill their time. The men of war educated themselves not only in martial skills but also the arts, philosophy and literature. New and uniquely Japanese art forms were developed and spread throughout the populace.

Artists embraced their new prosperous audiences, whose love for their works became synonymous with power and authority. Advanced road and water networks enabled many creators to move their artwork further afield, where it could be enjoyed and of course sold to a much wider audience. Trades such as weaving, ceramics, haiku poetry, kabuki, lacquerware and painting boomed.

As the infrastructure of the city changed to meet its peoples' needs, Edo witnessed the creation of buildings where people could shop and trade, namely Echigo-ya, the world's first - not to mention biggest - retail store (it employed around 300 people, making it one of the largest workforces at the time). Here one could purchase items such as kimonos, and its sales in the 18th century equated to approximately 10 billion yen in today's currency.

Business grew so rapidly that a new sales formula was introduced; no discounts, no mark ups and cash payment only. But the rules didn't just apply to buying and selling goods. There were strict dress codes for the merchants, who were forbidden from wearing embroidered silk in order to keep a lid on any social pretension and to curb any inflationary spending. Materials and designs were dictated, and citizens were even told when to switch to their summer and winter wardrobes. These rules could not be broken and even applied to the samurai, although they would try to flout them by dressing in disguise to attend events such as Kabuki theatre.

DRAMA IN THE BIG CITY

Kabuki was first recognised in the same year as the Edo Period began in 1603 with a show in Kyoto performed by a Shinto priestess called Izumo no Okuni and her troupe of female dancers aimed at raising funds for the Izumo Taisha shrine.

Early shows tended to be based on Buddhist prayer dances, their content of romantic tales intended to appeal to the masses. Kabuki's roots can be traced back to the 8th century and are a combination of music, dance and, above all, drama. Early Kabuki was often known for its vulgarity and lewdness. Originally, women played a part in popularising the artform, but they were later banned as many of the lead actresses were in fact prostitutes, and directors were concerned this would cause unwanted attention and possible fights among their male counterparts.

RIGHT Edo's premier retail store, Echigo-ya, boasted Japan's largest workforce (approx 300 people)

同二丁目
同三丁目
馬喰町二丁目
山口屋藤兵衛

Much of the inspiration for the performances came from the Kabukimono - gangs of urban youths who travelled in armed groups and generally harassed anyone who got in their way. Kabuki was hugely popular amongst the lower classes, particularly the merchants. The performers identified with the commoners, often using them for inspiration in their parts. Dried river beds also became a popular venue for performances, which included juggling and tricks by dogs and monkeys. Kabuki thrived during the period as it contained all the necessary attributes for a successful performance; music, dance, singing and most importantly a dramatic narrative. It is still recognised in Japan as one of the major classical forms of theatre in addition to Bunraku and Noh, and continues to entertain audiences today.

Despite Japan's strict social structure and isolation, the shogun created an area which came to be known as "the floating world", a licensed pleasure quarter that encouraged a newfound appreciation for the aesthetic and embraced hedonistic elements. This "floating world" assisted in fostering the creation of hundreds of varying artworks based around the environment. The culture inspired many techniques, including ukiyo-e, which is celebrated as one of the most famous artforms in Japanese culture.

A FAMILY TRADITION THROUGH THE AGES

A form of Japanese calligraphy, shodō is believed to be a direct expression of the writer's true nature, with the characters taking on their own art form and becoming one with the writer. Its early roots can be found in Buddhism, and it has been a fundamental part of education in Japan since the Edo Period.

Literacy at the time was impressive compared to other countries around the world and school attendance was high, with 86 per cent of children between the ages of seven and 15 in education. Reading and writing were taught, as was numeracy with the use of an abacus. Families paid what they could afford for their child's tuition as there were no set fees.

Shodō remains a way of life to the Japanese and is practised by people of all ages, with many families having their own set of tools at home. It remains a required subject in primary school and there are even shodō departments at many universities.

Over its 1,000-year history, shodō has undergone developments that are reflected in its changing styles, but the three basic ones are Kaisho, Gyōsho and Sōsho.

ABOVE A young woman practices calligraphy, a tradition that dates back for over a millennium

ABOVE Japanese ukiyo-e artist Hokusai's woodblock print The Great Wave off Kanagawa, also known as The Great Wave

PIONEERING PAINTERS

Woodblock printing (ukiyo-e) contrasted greatly to the story illustrations and religious images of the 16th century previously favoured by the elite. Before it emerged artists would have painted directly onto scrolls, rolled paper and folding screens. But with the introduction of ukiyo-e it was possible for pictures and images to be mass produced, allowing everyone to enjoy and obtain them. This form of art was one of the most popular of its time as it was created for the enjoyment of the masses, depicting both natural and urban scenes that were easily relatable.

The term ukiyo-e comes from a Buddhist metaphor that refers to the changing world of fleeting pleasures found in both the entertainment districts of Osaka, Kyoto and Tokyo, and the seasonal changes observed in nature. Famous for their bold composition, dramatic colours and calligraphic lines, these prints ranged from the dramatic and often violent to dignified and serene. Inspiration was taken from everyday pleasures and pursuits but also mythical monsters and make-believe characters. Originally used to transmit Buddhist scripture, polychrome woodblock printing was a convenient way in which to reproduce printed text. Images and whole pictures would be engraved on wood and pressed against paper to leave an imprint.

Originally the prints were only available in black ink, but later they were also produced using vivid colours. Nishiki-e printing is done by making an individual woodblock for each colour. The invention of the technique is credited to the engraver Kinroku and was popularised by the printmaker Suzuki Harunobu. These works of art are highly valued today - Dutch painter Vincent Van Gogh was a great fan and collector of ukiyo-e, even including some of his collection in his own works. Many other Western artists took inspiration from the abstract approaches to colour and varying uses of compositional space too. Ukiyo-e influenced later artists, particularly the Impressionists, to focus solely on the subject they were painting and disregard any complicated backgrounds. They also showed the beauty of a "flat" appearance in compositions.

Manga comics can also be traced back to the Edo period with some nishiki-e prints made during that period. The prints share qualities found in today's modern manga, which are all based around humour, satire and fun. It is also thought to have roots in the written language of Japan, which has numerous characters and symbols and is not easy to adapt to a movable type. Therefore it was just as simple to make wood blocks with illustrations and words rather than blocks featuring longer texts. These colourful prints had a raw, comedic and often biting element to them and depicted a playful outlook on everyday life, making them easy for people to appreciate and understand.

Long regarded as one of Japan's most inventive and visually dynamic painters and furniture designers, Tawaraya Sōtatsu is credited as being one of the co founders of the Rinpa school of Japanese painting (although it strictly wasn't an actual school but a group of artists notable in Japan for their outstanding artwork). These prominent figures included Ogata Kōrin (1658-1716), Ogata Kenzan (1663-1743), Sakai Hōitsu (1761-1828) and Hon'ami Kōetsu (1558-1637). It was Sōtatsu who brought the tarashikomi technique to the masses. This involves applying a second layer of paint to a piece of artwork before the first layer has dried.

TEA & TEMPTATION

The style of architecture during the Edo Period was called sukiya-zukuri and traditionally characterised by the use of natural materials in its construction - wood in particular. The design incorporates the aesthetics of a tea house, and due to its popularity the majority of buildings, both public and private, were constructed in this style. Katsura Rikyu (Katsura Imperial Villa) in Kyoto is considered to be one of the finest examples of traditional Japanese architecture. Built during the Edo period, it played host to imperial families and the social elite who enjoyed time there beside the Katsura River. Set in immaculately pruned gardens, it's also a superb example of Japanese landscaping.

Said to have been built to imitate Genji's Palace from classic work of Japanese literature *The Tale of Genji* (Genji Monogatari) - written by noblewoman and author Murasaki Shikibu between 1000 and 1012 and said to be the world's oldest full-length novel - the Katsura Imperial Villa was constructed using simple hardwearing materials and boasts not one but four teahouses, one for each of the seasons. Tea houses were originally used during the Edo period as a place for local businessmen and wealthy merchants to gather. Here they would be welcomed and entertained by geisha. It wasn't until the 17th century that geisha first made an appearance in the pleasure quarters of Osaka and Tokyo. The earliest ones were men called taiko-mouchi ("drum carriers"). They were tasked with charming the male clients using performances, conversation, service and a dash of sexual innuendo, much like their female counterparts went on to do in the mid-18th century when the profession became dominated by women.

By the 19th century geisha had risen to almost supermodel status, influencing popular culture and fashion and benefitting from a substantial income. Geisha lived in separate communities called "flower and willow worlds" away from other women who were either prostitutes or wives.

Appearance, particularly make-up, was important not just for performance but also for the women of Edo, and it can only be described as striking. The colour palette was made up of only three colours: black, white and red. A white powder was used for the face, while the teeth and eyebrows were painted black, unless a woman was married, then she would shave off her eyebrows. This was thought to hide any natural expressions. A product made from flowers called beni was used to colour the lips, and although when dry it would remain green, once mixed with water it would turn a

CLOCKWISE FROM TOP LEFT Woodblock printed books of the classic works of Japanese literature written in the early 11th century by lady-in-waiting, noblewoman and poet Murasaki Shikibu; traditional Japanese woodblock showing a woman in a highly patterned kimono depicting images of cherry blossom trees, bats, the moon and water while holding a book in her hands

vibrant red. Woodblock prints show women applying it and it is still made today using safflower. A good-quality jar could set you back around $100 US, so it would be wise to use it sparingly.

Fashion was another focus of the period, and what you wore again depended on your standing in society. Samurai, as you would expect, wore a kamishimo, a three-piece outfit featuring a long skirt with a split, outer coat and an inner kimono. Kabuki actors wore shirts that complimented the stage set they were performing on, and their vibrant and outrageous colours and patterns also held symbolic meaning.

Tokugawa rulers implemented strict laws on hairstyles, clothes and even make-up, using it as an effective way to control identity and establish another hierarchical reminder. Silk-woven garments were for the elites alone, as were bright colours. The lower classes wore garments made from hemp or cotton in shades of grey, brown and blue. Because of this division in both colour and fabric the nobility and samurai became the trendsetters for the proletariat.

Due to Japan remaining isolated for such a long period of time it became impossible to import goods from other countries. Japan had only a finite amount of resources, which were difficult to replenish. Specialised jobs were created in order to make the country self-sufficient and give everything possible a second life by recycling it where possible. Human waste was used to fertilise fields of crops, and people brought and recycled anything from candle wax, ash, barrels, and umbrellas to, most commonly, clothes and paper – only serving to make the artwork of this period even more impressive.

This era of prosperity and peace had a positive impact on the country in terms of an economic and cultural renaissance. One area that flourished was ceramics, with its production growing exponentially during this period. In part, this can be attributed to the number and influence of Korean potters living in the country at that time. New techniques were established and different materials and methods of production used. A new style of chambered kiln called a noborigama was used. This allowed for more precise control when using a higher temperature.

The discovery of deposits of kaolinite enabled the Japanese to use porcelain for the first time, demand for which surged with the introduction of the tea ceremony, a process that required new forms of ceramics for its rituals. Japanese pottery is still regarded as the finest in the world and tea ceremonies are thought to be a truly quintessential Japanese art form.

Another Japanese creation of the Edo period was lacquering. Those who mastered it could seek employment in Edo Castle, where they made furniture and luxury items. These items were a status symbol of wealth and power, and soon the daimyo and Tokugawa families began to place orders for lacquerware. Many prominent artists, including Koma Kyūi and others from the Rinpa school, gained further employment as goyō makie-shi (official lacquer artisans). They were tasked with crafting items like sword mountings and medicine containers. Other household articles followed as demand among the elite, samurai and merchants grew so much that items developed from small and practical to full-blown collections. Marie Antoinette was said to have been a huge fan and avid collector.

SCHOLARLY PURSUITS

Literature was readily embraced by a society equipped with new-found eagerness to read and study in a greater depth than before. For the first time Japanese classics were published in printed form, meaning that they became available to a wider and more diverse audience.

Printing had previously been reserved for reproducing Buddist writings, the classics only existing in manuscript form. Commercial publications started to take shape around 1609, and by the 1620s literary works were being printed for an eager public enthusiastic for more. Poetry was also popular, particularly haiku. This developed into an important genre, one originally called hokku and consisting of a mere 17 syllables arranged in lines of 5, 7, and 5 syllables. During the Edo period it was more of an opening verse, almost an independent poem whereby the

A BREW WAY OF LIFE

The tea ceremony remains a time-honoured tradition in Japanese culture. Rooted in the Buddhist principles of Zen, it encourages an appreciation of the beauty found in daily life and its routine. The tea ceremony takes place either in a designated tea house (cha-shitsu) or in a small special room or structure separate from the main house. The interior and decoration of the room hold great importance and care is taken when choosing both the decor and materials with which to construct it. Its aesthetic must remain simple yet welcoming, with an air of refined simplicity. At one end of the room is a small alcove (tokonoma) that will often have a flower arrangement and a hanging scroll displayed in it. There will also be a sunken fireplace used for heating the kettle. The entrance is through a small low door that has been designed to suggest humility. Everything in the ceremony is carried out in an established order, with the host bringing the utensils into the room, preparing and serving the tea and offering special sweets. Occasionally a light meal might precede the tea. Once the tea is finished, the utensils used to make it are carried from the room and the ceremony is complete.

ABOVE Adorned in their traditional clothing, these Japanese women are serving tea in a garden near Edo

writer had to include the time of day, season and any notable features of the landscape in only three lines. Thankfully today these rules are less regimented, making a haiku easier to construct.

Of the many great scholars of the Edo period, Buddhist priest Keichū (1640–1701) stands above the rest; his style and approach were well suited to the time. As a disciple of the academic movement Kokugaku, the Japanese school of philosophy and philology, Keichū's work set new standards in a country whose initial isolation helped to foster the development of provincial writing and renewed interest in the classics. He even undertook the task of studying and reproducing an edition of the Man'yōshū, the oldest collection of Japanese waka poetry. His aim was to reconstruct the work as closely to its original meaning as possible, no small undertaking. Many scholars went on to adopt Keichū's methods, continuing to produce further reinterpretations of the classics. Some notable examples were Kada no Azumamaro (1669-1736), and Motoori Norinaga (1730-1801), the latter publishing an incredible 30 works during his life.

With a rapidly expanding circulation, new and innovative genres began to emerge, and through booksellers, lending libraries and informal exchanges, writers and artists were able to connect and cater to a wider spectrum. Illustrated books became a medium of entertainment and artistic expression, helping readers to discover the wonders of science, distant places and religion. As with any sophisticated people, music played a central role in Japanese culture and was composed and performed in the larger cities. Tastes varied among the social classes, with music involving the shamisen proving popular with the common folk. This instrument (brought to the country in the 16th century) resembled a banjo and its three strings were plucked using a bachi, a sort of plectrum.

For their part, the samurai favoured Noh, a style of classical dance drama, while the court nobles enjoyed gagaku, an ancient court music. The shogunate boasted a bureau that oversaw and promoted visually impaired artists. It was these musicians and artists who played the koto, a zither with 13 strings and movable bridges, often in court settings and frequently as a cultural accompaniment for court ladies.

Jijuta ("song of monks") were composed and performed under the instruction of the Tōdōza, a guild for blind men. Members of the guild not only performed music but also worked as acupuncturists and masseurs. The shogunate was also partial to music played on an end-blown flute called a shakuhachi, which was only to be played by Buddhist priests of the Fuke-shu Sect.

Bucking the trend of its tumultuous predecessors, the Edo period afforded the Japanese a lengthy spell of peace in which a unique society skilled in countless crafts could blossom. In time, as the country began to turn its gaze outward to the wider world, its many styles and inventions were able to spread and influence previously unknown peoples in a myriad of ways. Modern society could learn a great deal from this chapter in Japanese history, especially the love its people bore for learning, their appreciation for nature, respect for family, commitment to recycling and reusing materials, and above all their pursuit of inclusivity.

CLOCKWISE FROM TOP Japanese kabuki actors wore a vibrant make-up that emphasised their dramatic expressions; Wealthy members of society regularly purchased nishiki-e prints, often in the form of calendars; Lacquered incense storage box made from cherry blossom, bamboo and pine, decorated with patterning that references the book *The Tale of Genji*

復興と革命
3

RESTORATION & REVOLUTION

A NEW WORLD BECKONS
SHADOWS FLEE ELECTRIC LIGHT
FROM DESTRUCTION, GROWTH

JAPAN'S CULTURE SHOCK

HOW COMMODORE MATTHEW CALBRAITH PERRY OF THE UNITED STATES NAVY OPENED JAPAN, SECLUDED FOR CENTURIES, TO THE WORLD

The United States grew by leaps and bounds across the North American continent during the 19th century. The discovery of gold in California in the 1840s helped drive American settlers to the Pacific Coast to make their fortunes. By mid-century, though much of the land in-between the coasts remained to be settled, the US had become a Pacific nation.

This opened new horizons for the US. Among the most prominent was the desire to possess a share of the lucrative China trade. Hitherto, the Chinese market had been dominated by European powers, such as Britain and Holland, that had been trading in Asia for centuries.

Japan came to figure in American plans. The US sought to strengthen its presence in the Pacific through the creation of government-subsidised mail steamship lines that would compete with British firms for dominance of the international mail trade. American mail steamers would pass by Japan, a mysterious and closed country of which little was known. It was clear that the island nation would be an excellent place to get coal, if only they would allow foreign ships into their harbours.

Another reason for seeking to 'open' Japan was the treatment of shipwrecked American seamen by the Japanese. American whaling ships had in recent years begun hunting prey in the northern Pacific,

and unfortunate seamen who had washed ashore in Japan had run afoul of severe laws that forbade foreigners, especially Christians. Those that got stranded in Japan were often roughly handled by Japanese authorities, who sought to insulate their country from all foreign contact.

Japan in the middle of the 19th century was ruled by a military government of samurai, called the bakufu, under the leadership of the Tokugawa dynasty in Edo (modern Tokyo). The shoguns had closed off Japan for over two centuries, refusing to have anything to do with the 'barbarians' beyond. Japan had developed culturally in the intervening period, but would soon learn that it had fallen drastically behind the West, technologically speaking.

THE JAPAN EXPEDITION

Top-ranking figures in the US government, including President Millard Fillmore, wanted to open Japan to trade. Several earlier attempts to do so had failed, for various reasons, primarily because of the unwillingness of the Japanese government to have anything but the most limited, carefully controlled intercourse with the outside world. This did not deter the Americans, who thought that a more determined, though peaceful, approach could achieve the results they wanted.

The US Navy chose Commodore Matthew Calbraith Perry, one of its leading officers, to command the Japan expedition. Perry was one of the best officers that the Navy could have picked to conduct the delicate diplomacy required. During his long career Perry had conducted negotiations with numerous foreign potentates on behalf of the US government, including in Europe, Africa and Mexico.

Perry had been instrumental in getting the ball rolling for the Japan expedition, having written to Secretary of the Navy William Alexander Graham over the winter of 1851-52 about the desirability of sending an expedition to conclude a treaty with Japan. Permission granted, he set about organising it.

Perry was to carry a letter from President Fillmore addressed to his 'Great and Good Friend' the 'Emperor'. The Americans were at this point only dimly aware of the position of the figure they would be dealing with in Edo, who was actually the shogun, Tokugawa Ieyoshi, ensconced in Edo Castle. The true emperor of Japan lived in Kyoto at this date. The letter expressed the 'kindest feelings' and requested an opening to trade and that shipwrecked US sailors be treated humanely.

PERRY'S FIRST VISIT, JULY 1853

Perry departed Norfolk, Virginia, in the steam frigate USS Mississippi on 24 November 1852, heading east across the Atlantic Ocean. The USS Mississippi rounded South Africa, taking on coal at Cape Town, then called in at Mauritius, followed by a stop at Ceylon (Sri Lanka).

Mississippi then sailed through the Straits of Malacca and called at Singapore on 25 March 1853, where she took on coal again. The Mississippi consumed coal at a prodigious rate, underscoring the need to have numerous coaling stations distributed around the globe, of which Japan, the US hoped, would be one.

LEFT What happened when the Black Ships arrived at Edo in 1853?

Passing next through the South China Sea, she stopped at Macao on 6 April, and later that day moved on to Hong Kong where Perry rendezvoused with the other ships of the US Navy's East India Squadron that he would lead to Japan. Perry's expedition would be the biggest that the US Navy had ever deployed.

The squadron moved on to Shanghai and then left for Japan on 16 May 1853. Perry's command was composed of four ships - the steam frigate Susquehanna, which he had made his new flagship; the Mississippi; and the sailing sloops Plymouth and Saratoga. Reaching Uraga, at the entrance of Edo Bay, on 8 July, Perry's squadron was greeted by two Japanese cannon shots that announced his appearance. Perry's vessels anchored a mile offshore and fired a salute with their guns.

The Japanese came out to the US squadron in small boats to take a closer look at the

TOP Perry encounters the shogun for the first time

LEFT Abe Masahiro, chief senior adviser to the Tokugawa shoguns

foreigners. Some carried artists who began sketching what they saw before them. Soon, their renditions of the barbarians from overseas were being churned out for eager public consumption by print-makers across Edo. Others were more militant in their reactions to the American ships, which would be forever known in Japan as 'Black Ships' on account of their colour. The samurai of Edo reached for their weapons, in case the foreigners were hostile.

Japanese soldiers and officials also went out to see the US ships, and tried to board, but the American sailors refused them access. One guard boat came up beside the Susquehanna, displaying a sign, written in French, telling the Americans to depart immediately. A Japanese, speaking Dutch, next told the Americans that a high-ranking official was in his boat and wanted to come aboard. The Americans replied that he would not be allowed to confer with Perry directly because, as the representative of the US president, the commodore would only meet with the loftiest of Japanese government officials. The official present, Nakajima Saburonosuke, was a lesser one, a mere aide to Uraga's vice-governor.

Contee told Nakajima that Commodore Perry had come to Japan bearing a letter from President Millard Fillmore to the emperor. Nakajima said that the expedition should instead go to the Dutch trade factory at Nagasaki and send the letter through that. Contee said no, insisting that the US expedition had arrived at Uraga precisely to be close to Edo. Contee also told Nakajima to withdraw the guard boats clustering around the American ships, or they would be made to back off. Most of the guard boats pulled back, and Nakajima left, saying the would return the next day, after conferring with his superior.

With Perry off Uraga, the Tokugawa bakufu tried to delay to gain time. Its diplomatic effort was in the hands of Abe Masahiro, the chief senior adviser to the shogun. Perry was to be told that the Japanese government would receive President Fillmore's letter at Uraga and that a response would be made in the spring of 1854. In the meantime, Abe started to devise a strategy to deal with the newcomers.

Another official, Kayama Eizaemon, arrived the next day, 9 July. Though Kayama was of a somewhat higher rank than Nakajima, Perry correctly deduced that he was still only a minor official, being just another aide to the vice-governor of Uraga, as was Nakajima. Perry refused to meet with Kayama directly, and conferred with him via his own subordinate officers. Perry's unwillingness to deal with anyone but a suitably high-ranking official was not mere stuffiness: it was imperative that he be seen as important by the Japanese. The message from Abe was that a high-ranking official would receive the letter from the American president and that an answer would be made via Dutch or Chinese interlocutors at Nagasaki in the spring.

Perry objected to this, and said that he would take it as an insult if the 'emperor' would not issue a reply directly to the US president's own representatives. Perry insisted that the letter must be delivered to an appropriate dignitary in Edo Bay. If it was not, he threatened to land an armed party and take it to Edo Castle directly. Kayama said that it would be eight days before a reply would be sent. Perry answered that he would wait only three or four days before he tried to deliver the letter on his own.

The Japanese agreed to a formal ceremony for the reception of the letter. On 14 July, Perry and a party of around 250 American sailors and marines went ashore at Kurihama, nearby to Uraga, where Perry handed over President Fillmore's letter in a wooden box to sufficiently exalted Japanese officials, a pair of aristocrats named Toda Izu and Ido Iwami. Once the letter had been formally received, Perry was told that he could now depart. Perry replied that he would return in the spring for an answer from the Japanese government, informing the Japanese that he would probably be bringing more ships with him.

FAR LEFT Sumo wrestlers were something that the Americans had never seen before

TOP LEFT The first meeting between the two nations' people

LEFT Perry's party meeting with Japanese dignitaries ashore during his second visit in 1854

THE COMMODORE RETURNS, FEBRUARY-MARCH 1854

Perry spent the interim in Asian waters before commencing his return voyage to Japan, which he reached on 13 February 1854. As he had suggested, Perry brought with him more ships to better overawe the Japanese with a show of American naval might. A new shogun now reigned in Edo Castle. Shogun Tokugawa Ieyoshi had died soon after Perry's departure, and had been succeeded by Tokugawa Iesada, his son. The Japanese had spent the past seven months since Perry's first visit attempting to devise a viable strategy to deal with the Americans. Abe Masahiro had sounded out leading Japanese opinion on the matter. Some wanted to maintain Japan's isolationist stance no matter what. Others wanted to open up a bit, while they used the breathing space to build up a modern military. By the spring, the Japanese authorities had already contracted builders in the Netherlands for two modern warships. Still others thought that international trade would be a good thing for Japan.

With Perry back in Japanese waters, two weeks were spent negotiating over a place to hold talks. They at last agreed on Yokohama, a fishing village not too distant from Edo.

Perry and his party of 500 men rowed ashore in 27 boats on 8 March 1854. A reception hall was specially built by the Japanese for the negotiations. Sailors, marines and musicians accompanied Perry ashore, where he was met by a delegation of five Japanese commissioners. Simply speaking to each other was extremely cumbersome, since Perry's English first had to be translated into Dutch, and then into Japanese. The Japanese had to have their words translated into Dutch, and then into English.

An official reply was delivered to Perry by the delegation's chief commissioner, Hayashi Naburo. The Japanese were willing to provide fuel, food and water to American ships and give aid to distressed seamen. Trade was not possible yet, but in five years a port would be opened to American ships. Until then, American ships could resupply with coal at Nagasaki. The Japanese informed Perry that they were ready to sign the treaty the next day.

But Perry wanted to have ports open to American ships designated forthwith. Meeting with the Japanese again on 17 March, the Japanese commissioners agreed to allow the use of Hakodate and Shimoda. Perry also pressed for a commercial treaty akin to the one that the United States now had with China, but the Japanese resisted. By 31 March 1854, the Treaty of Kanagawa, named after the prefecture where Yokohama was located, was officially signed by representatives of both nations, establishing friendly relations between the two nations, the use of Japanese ports by American ships, and guarantees of aid to shipwrecked American sailors in Japanese territory.

ABOVE Japanese woodblock print of Commodore Perry flanked by American naval personnel

JAPAN OPENED

Perry was acclaimed for opening Japan upon his return to America in January 1855, and he published three volumes of his memoirs. Perry's health failed him not many years after his return from Japan, and he died, aged 63, on 4 March 1858. The legacy of his voyage would long outlive him, both for good and ill.

THE COMMODORE

Perry was one of the US Navy's finest officers and a good choice to lead the Japan expedition

Commodore Matthew Calbraith Perry was a member of a famous American naval family. His father, Christopher Perry, of Rhode Island, had served aboard privateers during the American War of Independence and Perry himself had joined the Navy as a 15-year-old midshipman in 1809. His older brother, Oliver Hazard Perry, won glory for his 1813 victory over a British squadron at the Battle of Lake Erie during the War of 1812.

After the war's end in 1815, Perry found himself engaged in hostilities with Algiers and suppressing pirates in the Caribbean. During the Mexican-American War (1845-1848), Perry had commanded the American flotilla that had bombarded Veracruz, assisting in its capture by American troops. Perry earned the reputation of being a stern disciplinarian, but also that of an officer who was much concerned with the health of his crew, taking pains to protect them from the ravages of scurvy, malaria and yellow fever.

Perry possessed a keen intellect, and his skills went beyond the merely military. He was an avid student of nautical science and botany, and conducted diplomatic missions on behalf of the US in Africa, Turkey and the Caribbean during his many years at sea. He would be tapped by his superiors to run the Brooklyn Navy Yard in the 1840s.

Perry's diplomatic skills would be tested to the utmost by the Japan Expedition. He had to be conciliatory to the Japanese, since his mission was peaceful, but still firm and resolute in pressing the American position with the reluctant Japanese negotiators. It was a difficult balance, but one that Perry struck, a crucial reason for his ultimate success.

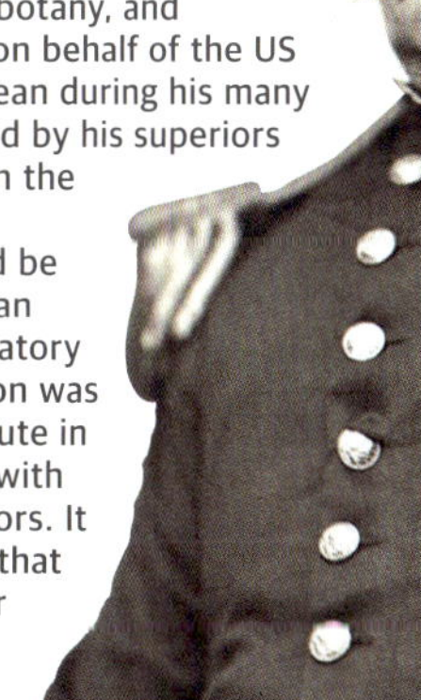

THE MEIJI RESTORATION

AN ERA WHERE JAPAN MOVED AWAY FROM TRADITIONAL FEUDALISM AND MODERNISED, TRANSFORMING ITS ECONOMY AND SOCIETY WITH TECHNOLOGICAL ADVANCEMENTS AND MILITARY DEVELOPMENTS

Change was in the air in the land of the rising sun. By the mid-1860s, Japan had been ruled by the Tokugawa shogunate for more than two centuries, but its time was coming to an end. The country was led from the capital, Kyoto, but the nation was regionally divided in a feudal system of hans where local samurai governed over their own territories. It was a new breed of young samurai who orchestrated a coup on the government and its leader, Tokugawa Yoshinobu. He was to be the final shogun of what is now seen as the end of traditional Japan.

A desire to overthrow the shogunate had been growing for years. The aim was to build a modern, united nation state and to increase Japan's influence on mainland Asia. It was thought that industrialising would build the economy and the military to match, and even exceed, the Western nations. The Tokugawa shogunate had refused international trade deals and had long followed a policy of isolation, avoiding trade relations with European countries, unlike its neighbours on the Asian mainland, China and Korea. This policy was broadly successful as its neighbours could be forced into trade agreements on unfavourable terms by gunboat diplomacy. However, as the Industrial Revolution boosted the economies, militaries and technologies of the Western world, many dissenting voices in Japan felt the country was being left behind and wanted a piece of the diplomatic action. This came to a head in 1853 when a squadron of US Navy warships sailed into Edo bay demanding access to Japanese ports, to which the shogunate quickly agreed to in an unequal treaty. These steam-powered vessels were vastly superior to Japanese ships, which had seen their dominance in the Sea of Japan slowly diminish over time. This show of power demonstrated how far behind in military technology Japan was and lit the fuse for a change of rule in the country.

Japan had been cracked open and more agreements, with few benefits for Japan, were made with other Western countries. These new, unbalanced regulations resulted in shortages of several important commodities in Japan such as tea and silk, increasing inflation. Cheap materials were hastily imported to cover the scarcity, which then affected the finances and success of homegrown business. This was the final straw for the anti-government forces and, in 1868, the country went to war with itself.

WAR & RESTORATION

The Boshin War proved to be the end of the Tokugawa shogunate. A two-year conflict on land and sea, the reformers were comprised of samurai from the southern Satsuma and Chōshū areas of Japan while the shogunate was protected by other samurai forces. Yoshinobu stepped down as shogun before he was killed and the

ABOVE As a clean break with the past, the imperial palace was moved from the old capital of Kyoto to the new capital, Tokyo

16-year-old Mutsuhito ascended to the throne and became Emperor Meiji. Yoshinobu did this to try and avoid war, but the reformers did not accept a completely peaceful transition of power and marched upon the Imperial Palace in Kyoto in a coup d'état. And so began the conflict.

The shogunate armies outnumbered their enemies who had one distinct advantage. Relations and dealings with external powers meant they had increased access to rifles and artillery than their opposing forces. This added firepower was crucial in the victory at Osaka Castle and the subsequent encirclement of the city of Edo by 50,000 troops. The main island of Honshu had been taken but northern territories in Hokkaido fought on under the banner of the Ezo Republic. Those still loyal to the republic dug in for the defence of Hokkaido as the last remaining shogunate stronghold. The use of modern weapons such as gatling guns and an ironclad warship secured the land and sea for the Meiji forces and the Ezo Republic was finally defeated in June 1869.

The mantra for the reformers was 'Revere the emperor, expel the barbarians' as it was deemed that the Meiji Restoration was a re-installation of the original imperial line – a democratic restoration rather than a revolution. It was far from a bloodless war with around 3,500 dead and wounded, but the transition of power was not as violent as the Russian and French revolutions. There was even an official period of mourning during the transfer of rule as Feudal Japan came to an end.

Mutsuhito was the first emperor to have a knowledge of international affairs and was determined to advance the country for the benefit of the people of Japan. Initially, due to his young age, he was closely supported and guided by supreme advisors. Mutsuhito maintained a symbolic yet active role as emperor during his reign. He was present at the completion of the first railway and put himself fully behind Japan's modernisation projects and military campaigns.

"JAPAN WAS MODERNISING AT A RAPID RATE BUT NOT EVERYONE IN THE COUNTRY WAS ONBOARD"

The reformers wasted no time in making the changes that they envisioned would bring unity, strength and security to the country. The capital was moved from Kyoto to Edo (renamed as Tokyo) as a symbolic cut of ties from what came before. Regional feudalism was abolished, as samurai relinquished their lands to governors installed by the new emperor, and replaced with full national rule and an administrative system that included nationalised free education. The new government aimed to improve the nation's literacy from just 40 per cent and the reformers had studied Western powers closely on trips to the USA and Europe. Impressed by the American industry and the power and structure of Bismarck's German Empire, these ideas were incorporated to build a newly-industrialised economy and a modernised society. The Gregorian calendar was introduced, as was a constitutional monarchy, and a switch from agriculture to factory industry. National identity was prioritised with Japan's native religion of Shintoism replacing Buddhism as the chosen state religion and national taxation and private ownership of land were implemented. This provided the emperor and nobles with the funds to build a conscripted national army to replace the previous regional

ABOVE Meiji means 'enlightened rule' in Japanese and Tokyo, which became the capital city, means 'eastern capital'

military units. Compulsory military service meant the emperor would always have a standing army to call upon in case of internal rebellion or overseas invasion. Japan was modernising at a rapid rate but not everyone in the country was onboard with the sweeping reforms changing the nation.

RESISTANCE TO THE REGIME

Early on in the restoration, the traditional Japanese class system was abolished. This meant the end of the samurai class, which had been a central part of Japanese society since the 12th century. Saigō Takamori was one of the samurai who fought against the Tokugawa shogunate in the Boshin War. He came to disagree with the rapid modernisation of the country, as samurai were forced to renounce their former lives and roles or fall into poverty. This came to a head in the 1877 Satsuma Rebellion. The six-month uprising was the largest revolt against Meiji rule and tested the new westernised, modern conscripted army. The rebellion ended in failure at the Battle of Shiroyama, as the new army's modern techniques and weapons proved crucial. Realising all was lost, Saigō committed seppuku (samurai suicide) and, with him, the power and influence of the samurai class was lost forever.

In addition to this more famous rebellion, the indigenous population of Japan's northern island, Hokkaido, were forced from their homelands. The Ainu were forcibly relocated to the mountains in the centre of the island as emigration of Meiji communities from the larger Honshu island pushed them and their culture away. Government forces seized control of the island as the Ainu people were slowly assimilated into Meiji ways and their traditional culture gradually disappeared. An act was passed in 1899 to protect the Ainu but this legislation forbode the speaking of the indigenous language and the recognition of its many traditions. These two instances demonstrated the purpose of the Meiji Restoration to make a clean break with the past, whatever the consequences. It would be an ideological precursor to the discrimination of Koreans under Imperial Japan in the early 20th century and is a dark cloud on the progress made during the period.

TRANSFORMING THE LAND OF THE RISING SUN

Japan converted from a predominantly agricultural country of self-governing regions to an industrialised nation with a powerbase centralised in Tokyo. This was down to a huge national infrastructure project that was implemented by the government. With a decreasing

THE IWAKURA MISSION

To help pursue their vision of a new modernised nation, members of the Meiji government travelled overseas for inspiration. The Iwakura Mission was an 18-month long excursion between 1871-1873 where Japanese officials visited Europe and America. It was successful in moulding Japan's future. Relations with France were smoothed after the country's previous support for the shogunate. The French contributed to the newly-expanded Japanese Navy, which was based on Britain's Royal Navy, while the army was Prussian in its setup. The new education system was a hybrid of the French and German models and focused more on Western ideals like individualism and social equality. Prime minister Itō also embarked on a fact-finding mission to Germany before he took up his appointment as PM. He was impressed by their show of power and imperial ambitions and was determined to replicate that in Japan.

The Meiji government also welcomed representatives from other countries to its shores. Foreign experts were welcome to examine the country and to teach and implement new ideas on society, economy and military. These specialists helped popularise exports of silk to the West and were paid much higher sums than their Japanese counterparts to provide the expertise that contributed to the modernisation of Japan.

ABOVE Members of the Iwakura Mission while visiting London. Japan was no longer in isolation and open to Western involvement and partnership

ABOVE Emperor Mutsuhito ruled Japan throughout the entire Meiji era, from a teenager until his death in 1912

importance of regions, people could now travel more freely to find work and the technology was provided for them to do so. The last spikes were driven on the country's earliest railways as the first steam locomotive in Japan made its inaugural journey in 1872 from Tokyo to Yokohama. 18 miles of track were completed that year and it increased dramatically to 7,100 miles by 1914.

Networks of telegraph poles, on land and undersea, were erected as Japan became more closely connected. Road networks were improved and buildings were increasingly constructed with brick rather than wood. Telephone lines were set up, shipyards and factories opened and extended as well as access to an increased range of consumer products. The law system was revamped and there was also a new nationalised postal service by 1871 where letters could be sent internationally. It was much more effective than then previous piecemeal courier method. Japan embraced its own form of Western capitalism and all this progress had to be fuelled by a workforce. Employees worked long, hard hours and, to make ends meet, and to boost productivity, children often worked as well. Former farmers were now working in factories with their children and it wasn't unheard of for them to die at work or be sold off for other labour.

Popular culture was a now a blend of traditional Japanese customs and Western practices. Red meat was a popular part of the standard diet for the first time and Ueno Zoo was opened in Tokyo in 1882. The wearing of samurai swords was banned as was the traditional samurai top-knot hairstyle. In 1885, Japan had its first prime minister. Itō Hirobumi oversaw the publication of a new national constitution in 1889, leading to more power for political parties, a cabinet system of government, a citizen-involved national assembly and the first elections a year later. Initially, only the richest in aristocracy could vote in this semi-democratic system but this was extended to all men in 1925 after the Meiji period had ended. Leadership was entrusted to a group called the Genrō who led the cabinet. Itō himself was a Genrō before becoming prime minister. A prominent Genrō was Yamagata Aritomo who also served as prime minister. A former soldier in the Chōshū forces that fought against the shogunate during the Boshin War, he had been impressed by the power of Western armies. This stayed with Yamagata and he commanded the Imperial Force (later renamed Imperial Guard) which later suppressed the Satsuma Rebellion. Yamagata was pivotal in building and shaping the modern Japanese army that was designed to march and invade. He oversaw the Japanese military efforts in wars against China and Russia later moved into politics and served as became prime minister from 1889-91 and again from 1989-1900. Under the Genrō and written in the constitution was the Diet. This comprised of two equal houses, The House of Peers and the House of Representatives, who passed laws. A tweaked version of this system is still in place today.

The nation's industry was overhauled into a capitalist system. This signalled the birth of wealthy family-run businesses called zaibatsu that called the shots across many sectors of industry and commerce. Some of these original Zaibatsu are still open for business today and they were cornerstones of Japan's economic growth in the late 19th and early 20th centuries. An example is Mitsubishi. The now popular international car manufacturer originated in the Meiji era as a naval troop transport. The firm worked closely with the national projects

ABOVE The Yasukuni Shrine honours the victims of the Boshin War. Its construction was ordered by the emperor and it now honours the fallen of subsequent wars

東京名所
版権所有
吾妻土産名所図画三
大村益治郎氏銅像

and stepped in when national transport initiatives were too costly to be constructed directly by the government. The system ensured that the government received a return on what it invested while providing public projects and promoting private enterprise. In addition, it was the decreasing agricultural sector that picked up the tax bill, rather than the zaibatsu. This model would later be replicated in Korea where companies like Hyundai and Samsung sprang up in the early-mid 20th century.

One sector of industry that boomed in the Meiji era was silk. Stepping into the breach when Italian silk experienced a shortage, Japanese silk began to be sold worldwide and boomed as the period continued, as did coal which was required to power modern industry and transportation. Japan itself isn't plentiful in natural resources due its size and mountainous forested terrain, but it punched above its weight with its silk and tea exports that were of high value in the West. This income was then spent on enhanced technology, to increase its exports even more, and then infrastructure projects to support military expansion as Japan turned its gaze to the nearby Asian landmass.

"JAPAN WAS ON ITS WAY TO BECOMING A MILITARY POWERHOUSE"

MILITARY MATTERS

The growth of heavy industry and a conscription law meant Japan was on its way to becoming a military powerhouse with colonial ambitions. Japan could enact gunboat diplomacy of its own against Korea as it expanded its sphere of influence into more areas. This expansion brought Japan into conflict with China as the First Sino-Japanese War broke out in 1894. The modernised Japanese forces defeated the Chinese with Japan gaining extra islands and mainland territories including Taiwan. This time, it was Japan's turn to implement a treaty on its terms. Despite Western powers interfering and insisting on the return of some lands to China, the victory was popular in Japan and prompted the signing of the Anglo-Japanese alliance in 1902. A couple of years later, Japan was at a war again, this time with Russia.

The outcome of the Russo-Japanese War of 1904 sent shockwaves across the world. Buoyed by its treaty with Britain and the part it played in containing the Chinese Boxer Rebellion in 1900, Japan stood up to Russian expansion in two areas it craved to invade and own, Korea and Manchuria. Victories at Port Arthur and Tsushima Strait inflicted huge losses on a shocked Russian Navy. The war ended with the US-created Treaty of Portsmouth as Japan reclaimed the Liaodong Peninsula and gained part of Manchuria as well as Sakhalin and the China Sea. Japan's newfound ability and confidence to take on and defeat a long-established military powerhouse like Russia suggested that the tides of power were changing. Japan went one further in 1910, taking control of the Korean Peninsula, shortly after prime minister Itō was assassinated by a Korean nationalist in Harbin, Manchuria.

The first ideas of Japanese Pan-Asianism in Japan emerged in the Meiji era. This was a belief that Japan would unite Asian countries and lead them to stay strong against Western expansion. This was used by some as the reasoning for Japan's wartime forays into China and Korea - it was a product of security concerns and not just imperialist aggression. If either were invaded by a Western nation, then Japan would much more likely be under threat. The wars weren't wholly popular with the Japanese people but the military gains and the belief in the emperor meant that any dissatisfaction did not turn into outright rebellion.

THE ASSASSINATION OF ITŌ HIROBUMI

The life of Japan's first prime minister ended in tragedy. In 1905, after stepping down as PM, he was the resident-general of Korea. At the close of hostilities with Russia, Itō was in the then Russian city of Harbin to negotiate the terms of the end of the Russo-Japanese war. Japan was in the process of annexing Korea, resulting in a rise of nationalism in the country. Ahn Chung-gŭn was a Korean who favoured his country's independence. Posing as a member of the press, he evaded authorities and waited at a railway station for Itō's arrival. As he disembarked onto the platform, Itō was shot three times by the gunman.

Fatefully, Itō was not fully in favour of Japan annexing Korea, and upon him being informed that the attack was politically-motivated, he is said to have exclaimed "He is a fool!". Ahn was sentenced to death.

The event resulted in a second treaty led by Russian leaders who were concerned that Japan would blame them for the murder. The moment still resonates now. In 2014, A memorial to Ahn was erected in Harbin, which is now part of China. This was criticised in Japan and remains a sore point.

RIGHT Itō was was honoured with a state funeral. The assassination partly motivated Japan to continue the annexation of Korea

A FOREVER-CHANGED NATION

The Meiji era ended with the death of its one and only emperor in 1912. The 44-year-span had witnessed a boom in technology, industry and economy. Japanese society was also overhauled, with the feudal system and the ways of the samurai long gone. It was now an outward-looking nation rather than a closed, isolated country. Literacy had doubled to 80 per cent by the end of the Meiji era and the succeeding Taishō era built on this progress. Society was more open and politics resonated and identified with, and involved more of the population. Cities grew and performing arts became more popular as more theatres and opera houses opened.

The success of the period, particularly on the factory floor and in the field of battle, set the scene for Japan's 20th century. Military victories and industrialisation gave the country a new aura of confidence that would influence its decisions in the Taishō era and beyond. Japan became a growing player in international trade and political affairs with and growing technological and industrial expertise. The Empire of Japan was established and the country would participate in both world wars, two more turning points in the nation's history.

ABOVE Japan's first ironclad warship served during the Meiji era. It fought against the shogunate at the 1868 Battle of Hakodate

BELOW Satsuma samurai in planning and conversation. Note their traditional haircuts and katana swords

THE IMPERIAL SHŌWA STATE

ACCESSION OF HIROHITO TO THE CHRYSANTHEMUM THRONE

25 DECEMBER 1926

25-year-old Crown Prince Hirohito accedes to the throne after his father's death, marking the end of the Taishō era and the start of the Shōwa era. Following his accession, the new emperor is not called by his name but is simply referred to as 'His Majesty the Emperor' or 'the reigning Emperor'.

DID YOU KNOW?

Emperor Hirohito reigned for over 62 years, longer than any other Japanese monarch in history

JAPANESE INVASION OF MANCHURIA

18 SEPTEMBER 1931

Following the false flag attack on Mukden, Japan launches its invasion of Manchuria. The attack is undertaken by the army without government authorisation but as it produces a swift victory, the civilian government has no choice but to support the army's actions.

OPENING OF FIRST METRO LINE

30 DECEMBER 1927

The section of the Ginza underground railway between Ueno and Asakusa in Tokyo is the first metro line in east Asia.

THE MUSHA INCIDENT

27 OCTOBER 1930

The Seediq people of Japanese Taiwan rebel against Japanese rule, attacking Japanese settlers. The Japanese response is as savage as the attack.

MANCHUKUO ESTABLISHED

1 MARCH 1932

Following the invasion of Manchuria, Japan establishes a puppet state, Manchukuo, in the area of Manchuria they control, settling it with imported Japanese.

1926 — 1927 — 1930 — 1931 — 1932

LONDON NAVAL TREATY

22 APRIL 1930

A treaty to stop the naval arms race is signed by Japan, the UK, the United States, France and Italy. However, it enrages ultra-nationalist elements in Japan.

ATTACK ON JAPANESE PRIME MINISTER

14 NOVEMBER 1930

Appalled by the signing of the London Naval Treaty, a nationalist fanatic shoots Hamaguchi Osachi, the prime minister. Hamaguchi dies later from his wounds.

THE MUKDEN INCIDENT

18 SEPTEMBER 1931

This Japanese false flag attack, in which a small bomb explodes under a railway line, is used by the Japanese army as a pretext to launch the invasion of Manchuria.

THE SHŌWA FINANCIAL CRISIS

1927

A financial panic strikes Japan. There is a run on 37 banks and many collapse, leaving the five zaibatsu houses dominant in Japanese finance. The crisis results in the fall of the government, led by Prime Minister Wakatsuki Reijirō.

15 MAY INCIDENT

15 MAY 1932

Ultra-nationalist elements of the Japanese navy and army launch an attempted coup d'etat, assassinating the prime minister, Inukai Tsuyoshi. The coup fails but the conspirators attract great popular support during their trial and receive only light sentences. Japanese democracy is failing.

DID YOU KNOW?
The Second Sino-Japanese War is sometimes called the Asian holocaust because of the Japanese war crimes that occurred

SECOND SINO-JAPANESE WAR
7 JULY 1937

The start of an extraordinarily bloody war between Japan and China that lasts until the end of World War II. It is calculated that between 15 and 22 million people die during the war, most of them civilians.

DID YOU KNOW?
The Tripartite Pact was signed by the Axis Powers to deter America from fighting against them

SIGNING OF THE TRIPARTITE PACT
27 SEPTEMBER 1940

The Pact was signed between Japan, Germany and Italy in Berlin. Under its terms, the signatories recognised each other's interests respectively in East Asia and Europe, and agreed to aid each other militarily should they be attacked by another power. The Axis was born.

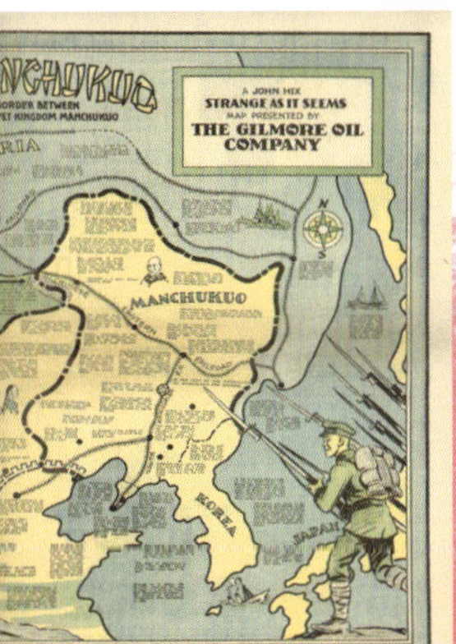

JAPAN LEAVES LEAGUE OF NATIONS
MARCH 1933

In response to condemnation of its actions in Manchuria, Japan leaves the League of Nations, entering a period of international isolation.

ANTI-COMINTERN PACT
25 NOVEMBER 1936

Japan and Nazi Germany sign a pact against the actions of the Communist International (Comintern). Japan hopes that this will develop into an anti-Soviet alliance.

NEW ORDER IN EAST ASIA
3 NOVEMBER 1938

Japan proposes a union of Japan, China and Manchukuo to defend against communism and to promote growth, under Japanese leadership.

1933 — 1936 — 1937 — 1938 — 1940

LEAGUE OF BLOOD INCIDENT
1932

Ultra-nationalist fanatics attempt to assassinate 20 businessmen and liberal politicians, and succeed in killing two. Their trial publicises their views.

NANJING MASSACRE
FROM 13 DECEMBER 1937

In the war's most notorious incident, Japanese troops murder and rape civilians in Nanjing, China, killing at least 200,000 people and raping an estimated 80,000 women.

FEBRUARY 26 INCIDENT
26 FEBRUARY 1936

Another attempted coup by young army officers fails despite the plotters killing two former prime ministers. The plotters are executed, but in doing so, the army is able to rid itself of the factions that were undermining its political aims. The end result is greater control of the government by the military.

GREATER EAST ASIA CO-PROSPERITY SPHERE
29 JUNE 1940

The New Order in East Asia expands to include Southeast Asia, creating a new political union using the yen as currency and with Japan in control.

WORLD WAR II

ATTACK ON PEARL HARBOR
1941
Hundreds of Japanese aircraft attack the US Navy's base in Hawaii. Over 2,000 American military personnel are killed and four battleships are sunk along with 188 destroyed airplanes. Japan then declares war on the United States, which proves a pivotal turning point of WWII.

DID YOU KNOW?
Germany and Italy declared war on the US after Pearl Harbor, eventually leading to their defeat

SINO-JAPANESE WAR
7 JULY 1937 – 2 SEPTEMBER 1945
Imperial Japan invades China in what is now regarded as the beginning of WWII in Asia. Tens of millions of Chinese and Japanese people are killed in the largest Asian conflict of the 20th century.

PHILIPPINES CAMPAIGN
8 DECEMBER 1941 – 8 MAY 1942
The US suffers its greatest defeat in military history when Japan occupies the Philippines. 23,000 American and 100,000 Filipino soldiers are killed or captured.

DUTCH EAST INDIES CAMPAIGN
8 DECEMBER 1941 – 9 MARCH 1942
The conquest of the Dutch East Indies is a great victory for Japan because their forces capture lucrative oilfields. This is a great asset and prolongs the war.

1937 — 1940 — 1941 — 1942

INVASION OF FRENCH INDOCHINA
22 – 26 SEPTEMBER 1940
Japan invades and occupies French Indochina after the fall of France to the Nazis. It's a precursor to later Japanese conquests of European colonies in the Far East.

TRIPARTITE PACT
27 SEPTEMBER 1940
Germany, Italy and Japan sign an alliance to deter the US from joining the Allies. However, its practicalities are limited with Japan operating almost independently.

BATTLE OF MIDWAY
4 – 7 JUNE 1942
The US Navy decisively defeats Japan by causing irreparable damage to aircraft carriers. This engagement is a turning point of the Pacific War.

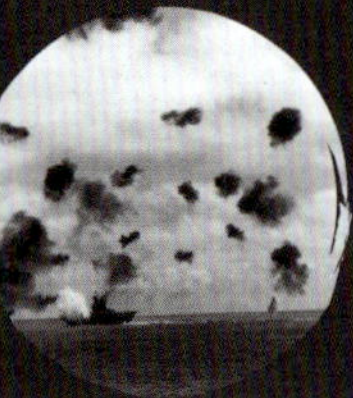

NANJING MASSACRE
1937
Japanese soldiers go on a murderous rampage after they capture the Chinese city of Nanjing. Approximately 40,000-300,000 captured Chinese soldiers and civilians are murdered, while an estimated 20,000 women are raped. Nanjing is a terrible foreshadowing of the widespread atrocities to come.

PACIFIC WAR
1941
Japan fights in the largest theatre of WWII against the Allies across Asia and the Pacific Ocean. Some of the largest naval battles in history take place in the Pacific in a conflict that is largely characterised by island-hopping campaigns, fierce engagements and extensive war crimes.

DID YOU KNOW?
Some Indian prisoners of war join the Japanese to fight the British in Burma

OFFENSIVES
1941-42
After Pearl Harbor, Japan launches successful offensives against Allied forces in east and southeast Asia. Simultaneous attacks are initially launched against Hong Kong, Malaya, the Dutch East Indies and the Philippines among others. Later offensives are aimed at New Guinea, Burma and various Pacific islands.

FALL OF SINGAPORE
1942
Japan achieves one of its most significant victories when Tomoyuki Yamashita's outnumbered forces of 36,000 soldiers capture the major British base of Singapore. 80,000 Allied troops become prisoners of war in what Winston Churchill called the "worst disaster" in British military history.

GUADALCANAL CAMPAIGN
7 AUGUST 1942 – 9 FEBRUARY 1943
Guadalcanal is the first major land offensive by Allied forces against Japan, lasting six months.

BATTLE OF IWO JIMA
19 FEBRUARY – 26 MARCH 1945
US forces win a bloody victory in the first battle in Japan. The capture of Iwo Jima's airstrips enables them to target the mainland for bombing raids.

SOVIET-JAPANESE WAR
9 AUGUST – 3 SEPTEMBER 1945
The Soviet Union invades Japanese-occupied areas of China and Korea. The Soviet entry is a significant factor in Japan's decision to surrender.

SURRENDER OF JAPAN
2 SEPTEMBER 1945
Japan unconditionally surrenders to the Allies aboard USS Missouri, bringing the final hostilities of WWII to an end.

1944

1945

BURMA CAMPAIGN
JANUARY – NOVEMBER 1944
British-led Allied armies force the Imperial Japanese Army to leave Burma after a series of offensives. The campaign is Britain's greatest military success against Japan.

BOMBING OF TOKYO
10 MARCH 1945
90,000-100,000 civilians are killed during a severe bombing raid on the Japanese capital. It is the most destructive single air attack in history.

BATTLE OF OKINAWA
APRIL 1945 – 22 JUNE 1945
The bloodiest battle of the Pacific War is fought on the island of Okinawa in the Ryukyu Islands. Hundreds of thousands are killed, including 150,000 Okinawan Japanese civilians.

SOUTHEAST ASIAN THEATRE
1941-45
The Japanese largely face British forces in this theatre, but campaigns are also fought against American, Chinese, Thai and Filipino armies. Most of the fighting occurs in Burma along with naval campaigns in the Indian Ocean.

DID YOU KNOW?
The US initially plans to attack five Japanese cities with atomic bombs, with Nagasaki reportedly replacing Kyoto

ATOMIC BOMBINGS OF HIROSHIMA & NAGASAKI
AUGUST 1945
129,000-226,000 people (the majority of them civilians) are killed when American aircraft drop two atomic bombs on the Japanese cities of Hiroshima and Nagasaki in August 1945. The bombings are the first – and they remain the only – use of nuclear weapons in armed conflict.

OCCUPIED JAPAN

THE ALLIED OCCUPATION OF JAPAN WAS IMPORTANT FOR NOT ONLY RESTORING THE COUNTRY BUT MAKING SURE THEY STAYED AN ALLY IN THE YEARS THAT FOLLOWED

Following the bombing of Nagasaki and Hiroshima in 1945, the United States occupied Japan and began to demilitarise the country and establish a new democratic political system. This was significant as this was the first time in history that Japan was occupied by another country. The person in charge of this enormous task was General Douglas MacArthur, appointed by President Truman. MacArthur pushed for Emperor Hirohito to be granted immunity from war crimes as long as he created a ministry that the Allies accepted. There was a concern that if Emperor Hirohito was punished in any way, this would cause the people of Japan to turn on the Allied forces and make the process of reforming the country tougher. After years of war, the majority of Japan's population was starving, so one of the first priorities was to provide aid to the people. This would prove to be difficult, as there were food and housing shortages due to the bombings.

The country created a new constitution that went into effect on 3 May 1947. Emperor Hirohito would still be in power, but the political system was westernised and the Emperor would be more of a figurehead with no political power. Article 9 of the Constitution of Japan stated: "The Japanese people forever renounce war as a sovereign right of the nation and the threat or use of force as means of settling international disputes." Japan would remove all of its land, sea and air forces, along with many military officers who were punished for war crimes and banned from moving into politics.

The Supreme Command of Allied Powers (SCAP) occupied Japan longer than expected due to the economic crisis the country faced. There was concern that a weak economy would tempt Japan to move towards communism. The Korean War in 1950 would end up being a blessing for Japan, as the country became the supply depot for American forces during the conflict.

This also provided essential assets for the United States when it came to monitoring Russia and Korea during the emerging Cold War. This change of priorities was called the Reverse Course. SCAP moved their focus to stabilising the country and its economy, and it also went back on some early policies, most notably allowing Japan to have a military presence, but only in terms of defence.

Before leaving, the agreement allowed the US to keep bases in Japan in return for a security pact. The Treaty of San Francisco was signed on 8 September 1951 between the United States, Japan and 47 nations of the Allied Powers.

MAIN Families line up to receive rations. These were irregular due to shortages across the country and limitations meant that most people couldn't get a full portion

RIGHT Japanese prime minister Shigeru Yoshida signs the Treaty of San Francisco, surrounded by members of his parliament and US Secretary of State Dean Acheson

FAR RIGHT General MacArthur and Emperor Hirohito meet for the first time at the US Embassy in Tokyo, 27 September 1945 Jurōjin and an accompanying lucky rat blessing a small child

OCCUPATION

NEO TOKYO

HOW POSTWAR JAPAN RECOVERED FROM ATOMIC BOMBINGS TO BECOME THE MOST HIGH-TECH NATION IN THE WORLD

On 15 August 1945, a week after Hiroshima and Nagasaki were levelled by the world's first nuclear weapons, Emperor Hirohito took to the airwaves to speak to the people of Japan.

"After pondering deeply the general trends of the world and the actual conditions obtaining in our Empire today, we have decided to effect a settlement of the present situation by resorting to an extraordinary measure… The enemy has begun to employ a new and most cruel bomb, the power of which to do damage is, indeed, incalculable, taking the toll of many innocent lives.

"Should we continue to fight, not only would it result in an ultimate collapse and obliteration of the Japanese nation, but also it would lead to the total extinction of human civilisation."

With that, Japan surrendered. Almost four years after it had entered World War II, 3.1 million Japanese civilians and soldiers had died, its stockpiles were exhausted and industry had been gutted. American general Douglas MacArthur was charged with overseeing an Allied occupation, with an aim of ensuring the country could never threaten the United States again. This would mean demilitarising and democratising Japan, but the Allies refused to "assume any responsibility for the economic rehabilitation of Japan or the strengthening of the Japanese economy". So how did the country rise from the ashes to become a greater industrial powerhouse than ever before?

TRADING UP

After the Meiji restoration, the government commissioned the building of factories and shipyards, which were sold to entrepreneurs at a fraction of their value. Pro-business policies were introduced and huge loans were handed out to private companies. The textile industry in particular boomed, and Japan was able to compete successfully with British products in China and India. By the beginning of the 20th century, Japan had emerged as a world power.

The country benefitted from the absence of European competitors on the world market during World War I, and exported more than it imported for the first time since the isolation.

Its economy suffered less from the Great Depression than most industrialised nations, with its GDP expanding at the rapid rate of five per cent per year. In the 1930s and 40s, Japan expanded its reach into Southeast Asia, seizing coal mines in China, sugarcane in the Philippines and petrol from the Dutch East Indies and Burma.

But this would prove too great a burden. The vast expansion spread Japan too thinly, and it underestimated how quickly the US would react to its bombing of Pearl Harbor in 1941.

World War II saw rampant inflation, and with all industrial efforts devoted to the military effort, shortages were rife. Air raids on its major cities by Allied B-29 Superfortress heavy bombers destroyed much of its industrial plants and infrastructure. Production ground to a halt, and the Japanese economy came to a virtual standstill.

BEYOND SURRENDER

For the first three years of the Occupation, the MacArthur administration pursued punitive measures that deliberately worsened conditions in Japan. Factories were dismantled, equipment was sent abroad as reparations payments, purge lists of top business managers were compiled, and "excessive concentrations of economic power" were identified. In particular, there was a focus on the dissolution of the zaibatsu - family-controlled, monopolies that passed from father to son, which had been at the heart of industrial activity within the Japanese empire. The Americans were suspicious of monopolies and restrictive business practices, which they believed were not only inefficient and prone to corruption, but anti-democratic.

But in a drastic turn of events, the orders were soon rescinded. With tensions between the US and USSR growing, concerns were raised that the poor state of the Japanese economy would lead its people to turn to communism. Dissolution of the zaibatsu was halted and $2.2 billion was given to the nation in financial aid. Major investments were made in electric power, coal, steel and chemicals.

Factories were rebuilt and equipped with better and more modern machines than before, giving Japan an advantage over even the victor states. The Japanese media dubbed this "the reverse course". Shigeru Yoshida was appointed prime minister in 1946, and his policies, known as the Yoshida Doctrine, stipulated that Japan should forge a close security alliance with the United States and prioritise the economy.

In 1949, his cabinet created the Ministry of International Trade and Industry (MITI) with a crucial mission to promote economic growth through close cooperation between the government and big business. The 'Inclined Production Mode' was adopted that focused industrial efforts on the production of raw materials including steel, coal and cotton. The recruitment of new labour was encouraged - particularly female. With the growing workforce, powerful new enterprise unions were established, and by the 1950s, union membership had skyrocketed. The annual wage negotiations between enterprise unions and workers, called shunto - translated as the 'spring wages offensive' - were key to boosting the low wages of the 1940s and improving working conditions.

THE MEN THAT REBUILT JAPAN

SHIGERU YOSHIDA

1878-1967

Prime minister of Japan from 1946-47 and 1948-54, Yoshida's pro-American attitude and knowledge of Western society made him a prime candidate for leader of an Ally-occupied Japan. His policies focused on strengthening the alliance with the US to provide military protection, as well as economic recovery.

JOSEPH DODGE

1890-1964

The president of the Detroit Bank was selected as General MacArthur's financial advisor during the American Occupation of Japan. The Dodge mission was to bring Japan's rapid inflation rates under control by imposing a regime of fiscal austerity to balance the Japanese budget, establish a single exchange rate for the yen, and abolish the black market.

HAYATO IKEDA

1899-1965

Previously Minister of Finance and Minister of International Trade and Industry, Ikeda was also the Japanese prime minister from 1960 to 1964. He has been described as the "single most important figure in Japan's rapid growth" thanks to his investment in technology and his income-doubling plan.

DOUGLAS MACARTHUR

1880-1964

After rising through the ranks to brigadier general during World War I, MacArthur was made commander of the US Army Forces in the Far East in 1941. He oversaw the Occupation of Japan, becoming its effective ruler. He reversed the administration's initial economic policies to turn Japan into an industrial powerhouse.

SHINJI SŌGO

1884-1981

The fourth president of the Japanese National Railways is credited with the creation of the first bullet train, the Tōkaidō Shinkansen. He resigned in 1963, the year before its inauguration, as the estimated budget was far lower than the final costs. However, his project revolutionised travel in Japan.

AKIO MORITA

1921-1999

Morita co-founded Tokyo Telecommunications Engineering Corporation along with Masaru Ibuka in 1946. In 1950, it sold the first tape recorder in Japan and in 1957, it produced a pocket-sized radio. The next year, Morita and Ibuka decided to rename it Sony, and in 1961, it became the first Japanese company to be listed on the New York Stock Exchange.

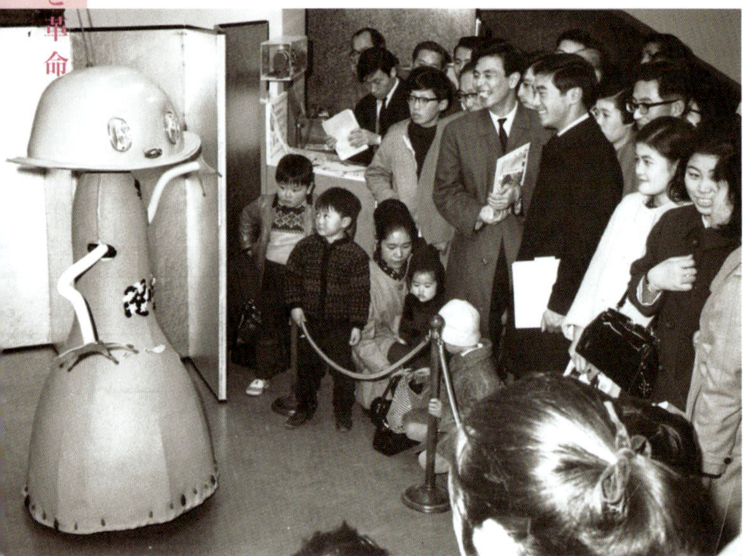

A system of shūshin koyō provided the security of lifetime employment in big corporations, allowing them to retain a loyal and experienced workforce.

But it was the breakout of the Korean War in 1950 that really set the gears of change in motion. The US needed somewhere from which to operate, and Japan was perfectly positioned to act as a military base. The order of mass firearms and other materials and services greatly stimulated the Japanese economy - so much so that Yoshida called the war a "gift of the gods".

These "special procurements" brought an estimated $2.3 billion into Japan between 1950 and the end of 1953.

Steel production increased 38 per cent in the first eight months of war and the automobile industry was revived - Toyota boosted its production by a whopping 40 per cent.

The San Francisco Peace Treaty, signed on 8 September 1951, finally brought the US occupation of Japan to an end. By that year,

THE BULLET TRAIN BLASTS OFF

Japan's iconic bullet trains (Shinkansen) were the first of their kind, an aerodynamic, innovatively-designed train that was capable of travelling at speeds up to 200 miles per hour. Introduced in 1964 (just in time for the Olympics that year), the first line ran from Tokyo to Osaka, and was an immediate hit with Japanese travellers. Cutting the journey time from almost seven hours to just four, passengers were delighted with the rapid ride, but it came at a cost of over 400 billion yen (almost $5 billion) to the Japanese government - twice the original estimate.

Far in advance of anything else in the world, the Shinkansen trains were symbolic of Japanese regeneration.

They supported the vision for a new Japan, with the metropolis Tokyo at its heart. To this day, most tracks on the Shinkansen network lead to Tokyo. However, the bullet trains are no longer the fastest in the world. China's Shanghai Maglev boasts that badge - but it only runs 20 miles, from the airport to the city's outer suburbs.

Japan has also recently introduced maglev trains, and in one test, they broke the land speed record for passenger trains by reaching a record speed of over 600 km/h. It's hoped these will serve the line between Tokyo and Nagoya by 2027, and will reduce the journey time by 50%.

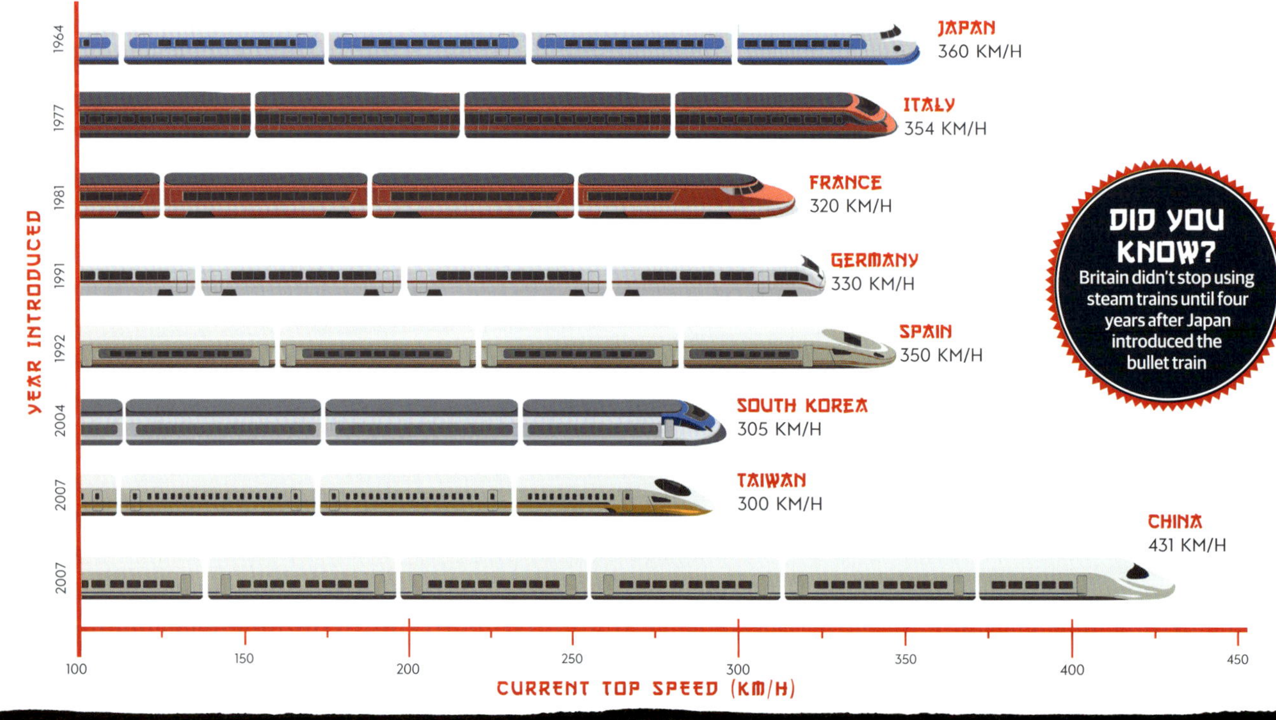

industrial production was back at its pre-war level. In 1952, Japan joined the International Monetary Fund and the International Bank for Reconstruction and Development, bestowing it with worldwide economic respectability. Incredibly, by 1955, production had surpassed pre-war levels, and Japan had become one of the first developed countries in East Asia. Hayato Ikeda was elected prime minister in 1960, and pursued a policy of heavy industrialisation. This led to the emergence of 'overloaning' – the Bank of Japan issued loans to city banks, who in turn issued loans to industrial conglomerates, who borrowed beyond their capacity to repay. This gave the Bank of Japan complete control over dependent local banks.

The companies formed from the earlier dismantling of the zaibatsu were reintegrated into a new business structure to create horizontal keiretsu – sets of companies with interlocking business relationships and shareholdings. Member companies held a small portion of the share in the other companies, which protected them from stock market fluctuations and takeover attempts. Not only did this allow for long-term planning, it also led to an attitude shift among Japanese managers, who began to tolerate temporarily low profits in exchange for better interest rates.

This new capitalism would prove to be more flexible and competitive than ever before, and capable of responding to even the greatest global economic and technological challenges.

THE GOLDEN YEARS

Ikeda's famous 'Income Doubling Plan' aimed to double the average personal income within ten years, and this was achieved well ahead of schedule. Throughout the 60s, household amenities such as refrigerators and sewing machines became more accessible, as did luxury items such as televisions, radios, cameras and air-conditioning. Personal savings rose, which in turn increased the funds available for industrial investment. While the consumption of daily necessities like food and clothing decreased, the consumption of recreational and entertainment activities and goods increased, including furniture, transportation, communications, and reading. Ikeda's government rapidly expanded investment in Japan's infrastructure, building highways, high-speed railways, subways, airports, port facilities and dams. This decade became known as the 'Golden Sixties'.

In Tokyo, by 1962 the population had exceeded 10 million, making it the largest city in the world. Two years later, it hosted the 1964 Summer Olympics. Enormous sums were spent on upgrading the city's infrastructure, including a new satellite tower to facilitate live international broadcasts. TRANSPAC-1, the first trans-Pacific communications cable from Japan to Hawaii, was also finished in time for the Games. The first Japanese bullet trains hit the railways and eight major expressways were approved. Two subway lines running under Tokyo's congested streets were also completed in time for the opening ceremony, and the port of Tokyo facilities were expanded to handle the traffic. The Olympics marked Japan's re-emergence on the world stage: the new Japan was no longer a wartime enemy, but a nation of peace and prosperity. But no sooner did Japan earn its place on the world stage that crisis hit at home.

FROM TOP TO BOTTOM The bombing of Tokyo during World War II cut the city's production in half; The Japanese Instrument of Surrender was signed on board USS Missouri in Tokyo Bay on 2 September 1945; General Douglas MacArthur stands beside Emperor Hirohito following the surrender; In the immediate post-war period, Japanese industry focused on the production of raw materials like steel; The first bullet trains were built to coincide with the 1964 Tokyo Olympics

In 1973, the price of oil increased from just three dollars per barrel to over 13 dollars per barrel. The following year, and for the first time since the war, a negative growth rate was recorded and inflation soared. During the second oil shock of 1979, oil increased again to 39.5 dollars per barrel. But the Japanese economy showed itself remarkably resilient. A special focus was put on telecommunications and computers. The automobile industry also boomed, with Japanese cars securing a third of the American market.

As of March 1980, the unemployment rate in Japan was below five per cent - an impressively low figure that would continue to drop throughout the decade and into the early 1990s. The austerity that defined the country during the immediate post-war period gave way to extravagance and conspicuous consumption. Life in 1980s Japan became one big, expensive party, with businessmen spending tens of thousands of dollars in Tokyo's restaurants and nightclubs and housewives sipping cups of coffee sprinkled with gold dust. It was also a period of increased international travel, as Japanese people went to the United States, Europe and Oceania in record numbers, shopping for Louis Vuitton and Gucci handbags, Savile Row and Armani suits, and the finest wines.

Anime and manga stole the limelight as the major forms of entertainment for the Japanese public, while Studio Ghibli, arguably the most famous and respected animation studio in Japan, was established in 1985. The decade saw the birth of characters like Donkey Kong and Super Mario Bros, and classic anime like Astro Boy and Akira. Nintendo came of age, offering video arcade games and their famous Family Computer (also known as the Famicom) video game system. American-based Atari struggled to compete - they couldn't defeat the Sega-Nintendo duopoly in the country's arcades.

Tokyo became a major financial centre, home of some of the world's major banks, financial firms, insurance companies, and one of the world's largest stock exchange, the Tokyo Securities and Stock Exchange. Soaring land prices meant that developers were forced to build upwards. For many families, this trend put housing in central cities out of reach. The result was lengthy commutes for workers, with many travelling for two hours each way every day in the Tokyo area. British newspapers reported on workaholic Japanese living in "rabbit hutches". Prices were highest in Tokyo's Ginza district in 1989, with some properties fetching over $1.5 million per square metre. A ¥10,000 note dropped on one of these streets was worth less than the tiny amount of ground it covered. Meanwhile, the Imperial Palace was said to be worth more than France.

The fun was not to last. With more people saving their income, loans and credit became easier to obtain, and with Japan running large trade surpluses, the yen's value rapidly increased against foreign currencies. While the Japanese stock market hit its all-time peak in 1989, the bubble burst in early 1992, and the period that followed would become known as the Lost Decade. Almost 30 years later, Japan has yet to recover from this period of great economic downturn. However, the island nation remains one of the most powerful countries in the world, and its cultural influence extends into homes, cinemas and streets across the globe.

FROM TOP TO BOTTOM Visitors line up to view a Mount Rushmore replica at the America Fair, Osaka 1950; The Toyopet S. Crown was Toyota's first export to the US in 1957; Factory workers do collective exercises, 1960. Working conditions greatly improved in the post-war years thanks to powerful unions; Pac-Man creator Masaya Nakamura is credited with masterminding the video game craze; Tokyo Tower, now one of the city's top tourist attractions, was built in 1958 as a TV transmissions tower

POP CULTURE SUPERPOWER

Japan's influence has spread worldwide

ANIME

One of Japan's biggest exports are its popular cartoons, known as anime. The hand drawings, featuring colourful characters and sharp lines, are a hit with adults and children alike. Storylines in comic books (known as manga), films and TV shows can vary from sheer fantasy to high drama. Anime has its origins in the Second World War era, but it didn't really take off worldwide until the 1980s. Then, in 2003, *Spirited Away* (by anime firm Studio Ghibli) won an Oscar for Best Animated Feature.

HARAJUKU'S CRAZY CLOTHING

Pay a visit to the hip, young Harajuku district of Tokyo to see Japanese adults and teens dress up in a huge variety of outlandish styles. It's like a non-uniform day at school, only more cliquey. There are loads of subcultures, ranging from Victorian Gothic-influenced dress to hip-hop inspired outfits. Though many of these styles were inspired by Western fashions, snappy Japanese wearers have incorporated their own traditions – which in turn are now having a their own impact on Western fashion.

JAPANESE POP MUSIC

You've heard of K-pop, now get ready for J-pop. Springing from the upbeat and extravagant music of the 1960s, J-pop is influenced by the sights and sounds of Japanese mega cities. It has since evolved into a plethora of different styles, including rock, punk, dance, and good old cheesy pop music. Young, uber-modern pop stars are idolised by their fans. Recently, bands such as Momoiro Clover Z have had global success, collaborating with US rock band Kiss.

VIDEO GAMES

Japan's affinity for technology and entertainment combined to produce an unstoppable force. Originating in the neon lights of 1980s Tokyo arcades, gamers poured money into the slots of Japanese-made machines, hoping to get the next top score. More recently, gaming fans have been able to take this form of entertainment home. Japanese games consoles such as Sega, Nintendo and PlayStation have long dominated the market.

KARATE

This old martial art was spread to the West as early as the 1940s, when the US army began incorporating it into their hand-to-hand combat training. After the war, Japanese masters were soon crossing the Pacific in force, as movies showcasing the grace and skill of Asian martial arts created a surge in popularity. The craze spread to Europe, too, particularly in Britain where people set up karate clubs – with the help of Japanese instructors – all over the country.

CULINARY DELIGHTS

There's more to Japanese food than sushi, but it's a good place to start. The innovative style of dining – featuring small plates of intricately presented dishes, usually involving rice and seafood – spread to the West in the 20th century. Perhaps the most famous hybrid is the 'California roll', featuring Japanese rice and seaweed, but with a distinctly American twist – avocado. Now, you'll find sushi in your local supermarket, and Japanese restaurants are widespread.

KARAOKE

Though it's associated with bad X Factor wannabes in dingy pubs, Japanese karaoke goes far beyond the realm of the amateur. Instrumental versions of songs are played, with their lyrics displayed on a screen, while you sing your heart out. In Japan, you can indulge yourself in a variety of ways – in a booth to yourself, or with your friends in specially designed karaoke boxes. It's taken pretty seriously, and karaoke rooms can even be found in the most genteel of establishments.

THE 'KAWAII' CRAZE

Meaning 'cute' or 'adorable', the love of things that make you go "awwww" is strong in Japan. 'Kawaii' designs usually incorporate sweet animals, wide-eyed characters, and bright, child-like colours. As well as buying 'kawaii' products such as clothing and makeup, a person can even act 'Kawaii' by exaggerating their innocence and naivety. Perhaps the most famous brand is Hello Kitty. Hello Kitty has featured on everything from jumbo jets to dim sum restaurants.

A TIME OF PEACE

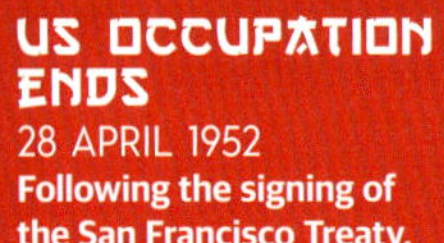

US OCCUPATION ENDS
28 APRIL 1952

Following the signing of the San Francisco Treaty, Japanese sovereignty is formally restored and Allied occupation ends. However, 260,000 US soldiers remain stationed in Japan, with many more on Okinawa. This leads to growing popular protests in the following decades.

ANPO PROTESTS 1959/60

Continuing resentment at the large number of US military personnel stationed in Japan produces popular protests that bring hundreds of thousands of people onto the streets of Tokyo. In June 1960, the protestors surround the National Diet (parliament) in Tokyo for days on end.

JAPAN JOINS UNITED NATIONS
18 DECEMBER 1956

Japan's entry into the United Nations is greeted with popular support while the Japanese government hopes membership will help reduce its dependence upon the United States.

JAPAN'S GROWING ECONOMY 1968

During this year, Japan overtakes West Germany to become the second largest economy in the world, after the United States.

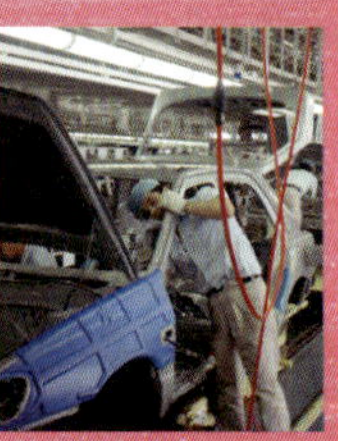

JAPAN'S CAR INDUSTRY NUMBER ONE
1980

Japan's car industry becomes the largest in the world, surpassing that of the United States. It retains that position until 1995.

1950 — 1960 — 1970 — 1980

JAPAN'S NEW ARMED FORCES
1 JULY 1954

Under its post-war constitution, Japan's new armed forces can only be used in defence of Japan: they are named Self-Defense Forces.

START OF TOKYO OLYMPIC GAMES
10 OCTOBER 1964

This is the first Olympic Games to be held in Asia. It is also the first to have events broadcast via satellite. Japan comes third in the medal table.

OKINAWA RETURNS TO JAPANESE CONTRO
1971-1972

The United States returns the prefecture of Okinawa to Japan. Okinawa was the only Japanese island to be invaded during World War II.

LIBERAL DEMOCRATIC PARTY IS FOUNDED
15 NOVEMBER 1955

Called Jiyū-Minshutō in Japanese, this conservative and nationalist political party has been in charge of Japan for almost all the post-war era. It is a broad conservative alliance, split into factions which struggle for political control. Some are moderate, while others are more right-wing.

FIRST SHINKANSEN RAILWAY OPENS

1 OCTOBER 1964

Japan's signature high-speed railway line begins service on the line between Tokyo and Osaka in time for the opening of the Tokyo Olympic Games. By 1976, it has carried a billion passengers. The first trains reach 130mph (210km/h). Now speeds of 200mph (320km/h) are common.

DID YOU KNOW?

The Shinkansen railway lines never interlink with local services, ensuring bullet trains are not delayed by slower locomotives

JAPANESE TSUNAMI

11 MARCH 2011

A magnitude 9.1 earthquake 45 miles (72km) east of Japan triggers a tsunami that devastates eastern Japan. Waves reach 40.5 metres (133 feet) and speeds of 700km/h (435mph), surging up to 10km (6 miles) inland. 19,759 people die and 2,553 are never found.

DID YOU KNOW?

There were no fatalities during the Fukushima nuclear accident despite the tsunami destroying all the reactor's backup energy sources

DEATH OF EMPEROR HIROHITO

7 JANUARY 1989

The longest-reigning emperor of Japan dies, bringing an end to the Shōwa era after six decades.

FIFA WORLD CUP

31 MAY – 30 JUNE 2002

Japan and South Korea jointly host the 17th FIFA World Cup. Japan win their group but are knocked out by Turkey, 1-0. Brazil wins its fifth World Cup.

EMPEROR AKIHITO ABDICATES

30 APRIL 2019

Emperor Akihito abdicates at the age of 87. He is the first Japanese emperor to abdicate rather than die as reigning monarch.

1990 — 2000 — 2010

END OF JAPANESE ASSET PRICE BUBBLE

1991

Between 1986 and 1991, property and stock prices in Japan become hugely inflated, producing an economic bubble. The bubble bursts in 1991, leading to Japan's 'Lost Decades' of low economic growth.

JAPAN HIT BY GREAT RECESSION 2008

The global Great Recession produced by the global financial crisis hits Japan hard, with its gross domestic product dropping almost ten per cent.

TOKYO SKYTREE

29 FEBRUARY 2012

The third tallest tower in the world is completed in Japan's capital. The Tokyo Skytree is 634 metres (2,080 feet) high. It serves as a broadcasting and observation tower.

TOKYO UNDERGROUND ATTACK

20 MARCH 1995

Members of the Aum Shinrikyo cult release nerve gas on three lines of the Tokyo underground, killing 14 and severely injuring 50. Japanese police hunt down the cult leaders, arresting 200. In the subsequent trial, cult leaders are found guilty and 13, including cult leader Shoko Asahara, are later executed.

START OF HEISEI ERA

7 JANUARY 1989

Following the death of his father, Emperor Hirohito, Crown Prince Akihito ascends the Chrysanthemum Throne. He is the first Crown Prince to marry a commoner, Michiko Shōda. His reign is known as the Heisei era. 17 prime ministers serve under Emperor Akihito.

DID YOU KNOW?

Shoko Asahara, leader of the Aum Shinrikyo cult, wanted to overthrow the government and install himself as Emperor of Japan

THE WORLD STAGE

JAPAN'S POP CULTURE IS TRULY UNIQUE. WE LOOK AT THE VIDEO GAMES, MOVIES, ANIME AND MORE THAT HAVE GONE WORLDWIDE

Oscar Wilde wrote in 1889, "The whole of Japan is pure invention. There is no such country, there is no such people". That observation is as true now as it was then. It's hard to think of another country that has managed to enter the pop culture bubble of the West the way that Japan has. We are currently living in a japanified world. Many of the electronics we use in our everyday life, the films we watch and much of the food we consume were either invented, improved or innovated in Japan. And many characters from Japanese media are icons around the globe: Pikachu, Hello Kitty, Gudetama, Sailor Moon, Ultraman, Super Mario, Astro Boy, Sonic the Hedgehog and Godzilla to name a few. And these all come from various different types of media. Japanese video games, movies, manga and more are enjoyed by people of all ages across the globe, but this isn't a new phenomenon, and it didn't happen overnight. It has taken time for this to happen but today anime is on the front page of streaming services, it's an event when a Japanese role-playing game like Final Fantasy is released and dishes originating from the country can be found on supermarket shelves around the world.

While Bollywood and K-Pop have made their way into the Western consciousness, neither India or Korea have managed to have the vast cultural reach that Japan has. Japan has a long and unique cultural heritage which has contributed to their one-of-a-kind perspective when it comes to storytelling and folklore, which has gone on to influence the media created in the country today. Japanese culture also has an attention to detail, high quality and unique creativity that is unlike any other country. It also helps that Japanese society has never had any stigma around watching animated shows or dressing certain ways, like cosplaying, and this has helped these subcultures flourish.

Let's start with Hello Kitty, perhaps the biggest export of Japan. The character first appeared on a coin purse in 1975. Yuko Shimizu purposefully avoided giving the cat a mouth so audiences could project onto the character, and it worked. Hello Kitty can be described as 'kawaii', the Japanese word for cuteness and this craze for all things cute came just as Hello Kitty emerged. The character is on plushies, comics, films, clothing, toys, stationary and just about anything you can think of. Hello Kitty has also been appointed as an ambassador of tourism by the Japanese Governments.

ELECTRONICS

As the economy grew post-war, Japan became known as the manufacturer of consumer electronics. Manufacturers produced cars, stereos, TVs and more that were of a high quality yet reasonably priced. The Walkman, a portable cassette player with headphones made by Sony in 1979, was revolutionary as it made music mobile. The device was so popular that the term 'walkman' became synonymous with mobile audio devices. Japan's share of the electronics market has declined since its peak due to competition from countries such as China, but we still see many of these devices as being 'Made in Japan.'

It's hard to see a video game industry without Japan's contributions. Space Invaders and Pac-Man flooded arcades and were so popular in Japan that rumours circulated that there was a coin shortage in the country. In the United States Buckner & Garcia had a top ten hit in 1981 with their song 'Pac-Man Fever.' Shortly after this came the North American video game crash of 1983, but at this time Japan was about to start a boom period of its own. Nintendo and Sega changed the landscape of electronic entertainment with their home consoles that took gaming away from computers and made them something anyone could pick up and play. Nintendo went a step further and introduced the world to the Nintendo Game Boy in 1989, making the video games that people of all ages enjoyed portable. Even some video game creators such as Shigeru Miyamoto became celebrities. As Western tastes have evolved over recent years to favour battle royales and first-person shooters, developers in America and Europe have grown to cater to those markets., while in Japan, mobile games are far more popular with audiences. This has led to an immense drop in Japan's market share of the software side of the video game industry, however on the hardware side of the business, it is still strong. Nintendo hasn't lost favour however, it is just as massive and culturally relevant now as it was back in the 80s, and Sony is a giant in the industry with its PlayStation consoles in the homes of gamers around the world.

Karaoke may be a joke to many, where drunk wannabe singers yell into a microphone, but in Japan there isn't a stigma and it's a common thing to do on a night out. Daisuke Inoue invented a version of what

RIGHT Hello Kitty is over 40 years old and is recognised all around the world as a symbol of Japanese pop culture

adidas
adidas
JFA

LEFT Akira Kurosawa's *Seven Samurai* is one of the most influential films in cinema history, being referenced or reworked countless times

we now know as the karaoke machine in 1971. It featured reverb to help those who weren't perfect singers and it played songs in different keys to suit different vocal ranges. While Inoue continued to develop and release more of his machines, companies began producing their own machines, filling bars and clubs around Japan. In the 1980s businesses set up specifically for karaoke sprung up. People could now rent their own room with a machine to have private parties or enthusiasts could get a solo box room. Screens were also introduced, displaying the lyrics on the screen with a video playing.

TV, FILM AND SPORT

In the 1950s Japan's demand for entertainment was high and this led to what many believe to be the golden age of Japanese cinema. Akira Kurosawa made numerous films that are considered classics such as *Rashomon*, *Ikiru* and *High and Low*. His films ranged in genres but he may be best known for his samurai films like *Yojimbo* and *Seven Samurai*. These would then be reinterpreted in Hollywood, often as cowboy films, with *Yojimbo* being reimagined in the West as *Django* and *Seven Samurai* as *The Magnificent Seven*. Even George Lucas has acknowledged that *The Hidden Fortress* was a heavy influence for *Star Wars*. While these films were loved by film buffs in the West at the time, monster movies were the first films from Japan to become popular abroad. This sub-genre of giant monsters fighting each other or destroying cities is known as 'kaiju.' In 1954 *Gojira* hit cinema screens in Japan and two years later it would have new scenes shot featuring Western actors to tailor it for American tastes, releasing in the West as *Godzilla*. It struck a chord with audiences as the film was an allegory for nuclear war as the nuclear reptile destroyed Tokyo. The film used miniatures and effects unlike anything cinemagoers had seen before. Actors wore giant suits and would walk amongst miniature buildings to give the illusion of height. The suits allowed for more realistic movement as opposed to other effects such as stop-motion. The character of Godzilla became an instant superstar. America had its own kaiju star with King Kong and in 1962 the two

RIGHT *My Neighbor Totoro*, about two sisters living in rural Japan who find wood spirits near their house, is the poster child for Studio Ghibli

ABOVE Super Mario is the most recognisable video game character and has appeared in over 200 games since he first appeared in 1981

cultural icons would clash in *King Kong vs Godzilla*, where they fought on Mount Fuji. There have been 33 films produced by Toho, the original distributor, five films made in America, and there are still Godzilla movies being made today.

The first animated film from Japan was made around 1917 but it wasn't until *Astro Boy* hit TV screens across the country in 1963 that animation became a hit with audiences. Anime would grow in popularity in the 60s and 70s with the likes of the baseball drama *Stars of the Giants* and space opera *Gundam*, about soldiers fighting from inside giant robot suits, but it wasn't until the 1990s that the west would come to love the art form. *Akira*, the film set in a dystopian Neo Tokyo in 2019, is credited as being the first commercially successful anime film in the West and this would lead to others being released such as *Ghost in the Shell*. On TV, *Dragon Ball Z* drew in audiences with its over-the-top fight scenes but the door blew open for anime in the western world when *Pokémon* arrived in 1997. *Sailor Moon* showed audiences of the time that anime wasn't just for boys, as its all-female group of superheroes featured a mix of humour, action and emphasis on friendship that wasn't seen in other shows.

While anime films did see Western releases, they were considered cult films until 2001 and the release of Studio Ghibli's *Spirited Away*. Directed by Hayao Miyazaki and deeply rooted in Japanese folklore, it follows a ten-year-old girl as she works at a resort for gods and spirits. It became Japan's highest grossing film, a record it would hold for almost 20 years, and it would get recognition around the world, winning an Academy Award for Best Animated Feature.

It's impossible to talk about anime films or even Japanese cinema and not mention Studio Ghibli. To put it simply, Ghibli is like a Japanese Disney. Their characters such as Totoro, Ponyo and Kiki are iconic and their stories have touched the hearts of people of all ages. It seemed almost fitting then when in 1996 the Walt Disney Company formed a partnership with Studio Ghibli's parent company, so Walt Disney Studios would have distribution rights to the Ghibli films.

With the success of anime in the 90s, many viewers would reach out to find more content from the shows they loved and this would lead them to discovering manga. Many popular anime are adaptations of comics known as manga. These cover a wide range of subjects, cater to all age groups and come in a variety of art styles. Drama, horror, sport, fantasy, sci-fi, romance are just a few of the popular genres. *One Piece*, the story of Monkey D Luffy as he tried to become the

TOKYO'S ELECTRIC TOWN

Akihabara, also called Akiba, is Tokyo's capital for all things anime, manga, video games and electronics. Located in central Tokyo, the district got the nickname 'Electric Town' after World War II when it became the place to go when buying electrical goods. In the 70s and 80s visitors from abroad would come to see the future of electronics with its state-of-the-art gadgets and appliances on show but as the rest of the world has caught up, Akihabara has evolved. The area is also changing physically with old buildings being torn down and new, tall, vibrant structures being constructed seemingly all the time. Today the district is less about household appliances or small stalls selling electronic components and more geared towards those interested in anime and gaming, or as some call it 'otaku' culture. Young women dressed as maids can be found on every street promoting nearby cafes, arcades are around every corner and there are countless stores selling figures, books and video games both new and old. Akihabara doesn't necessarily have sights to see, but wandering the main streets and the small side alleys offers an experience you cannot get elsewhere in Tokyo.

ABOVE The bright lights of Akiharaba's many arcades. These are packed floor to ceiling with all kinds of video games

King of the Pirates, is Japan's best-selling manga. It started in 1997, is still going today, has been adapted into a highly successful anime, and Netflix has produced a live-action adaptation.

The martial art karate made its way to the West post-war when the US Army added it to their hand-to-hand combat training. Soldiers stationed in Japan would open schools after they moved back to the US. The sport was included in the 1964 Tokyo Olympics, introducing it to the world, and shortly after martial arts films found mainstream success, propelling the popularity of karate. Japanese masters would travel the world, introducing the sport to various countries.

Sumo is one part religious ceremony, and another part sport. For a country with a population stereotypically uniformly slim, the hefty sumos in their loincloths are a striking sight. While sumo is not competed in across the globe like Japan's other favourite sports, football and baseball, it has made sporadic appearances on televisions in foreign countries as Channel 4 in the UK broadcast tournaments in the 1990s.

As with most cultural phenomena in Japan, professional wrestling was adopted and then given a twist that only the Japanese can do. Pro wrestling, known in Japan as puroresu, grew in the 1950s in the post-war period when American wrestlers would fly over, face the local talent and then more often than not, lose. This helped many people work through any animosity they had towards America. The matches were broadcast on NHK, the country's national network, and reached huge audiences. It was reported that when Rikidozan faced Lou Thesz in a televised bout, 87 per cent of televisions in Japan tuned in to watch. Rikidozan became a hero to post-war Japan and would go on to star in movies, much like Dwayne 'The Rock' Johnson has done so in Hollywood today. Female pro wrestlers, known as joshi, would surge in popularity in the 1970s and many were as well-known as the pop stars of the time. Some joshi would even release singles and EPs. Today the puroresu scene is diverse with promotions across the country and with their own niches. New Japan Pro Wrestling is the largest company, hosting shows around the world, and it has an annual tradition of hosting a show every year at the 55,000 seat Tokyo Dome.

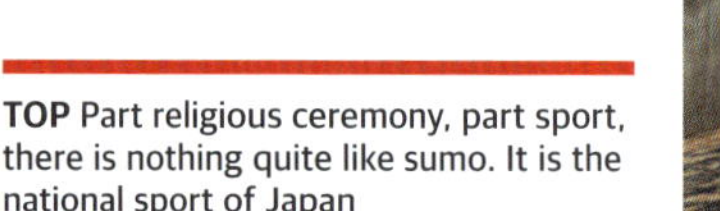

TOP Part religious ceremony, part sport, there is nothing quite like sumo. It is the national sport of Japan

ABOVE RIGHT AKB48 is Japan's most popular pop idol group, selling over 60 million records. The group has had 335 members since it began

RIGHT Japanese curries are often served with rice and a pork or chicken cutlet. They aren't spicy but are full of flavour

JAPAN'S STREET FASHION

Fashion grew in post-war Japan as its youth embraced clothing that took influence from America and Europe, and it followed their trends throughout the 50s, 60s and 70s. In the 80s the youth of Japan started to develop their own fashion trends that were distinct and unique to the country. The clothing company Uniqlo opened its first store in 1984, offering affordable clothing of high quality, featuring simple styles with muted colours. In contrast, the Lolita trend grew in popularity in the 90s as Uniqlo expanded across the country. Inspired by Victorian clothing, Gothic Lolita combined black, white and grey petticoats with macabre images such as skulls, bats and other gothic imagery. A subgroup that grew from this is Sweet Lolita, adding bright pink and kawaii imagery to the Victorian clothing. Meanwhile, the Harajuku district of Tokyo became the go-to place for finding the new trends. The streets are filled with boutiques offering eccentric, colourful and outrageous clothing that cater to the various subcultures gathering in the district. Another trend that rose in the 1990s was cosplay, people dressing as their favourite characters from anime and video games. Kimonos and yukatas, the traditional Japanese garments, are still worn today in the summer and on ceremonial occasions.

ABOVE Harajuku is full of boutique shops offering all kinds of fashion trends from gothic to cyberpunk and everything in between

MUSIC

The music of Japan hasn't been able to pierce the West like Korea has managed, but Japanese artists have had hits abroad. In 1961 Kyu Sakamoto's single 'Ue o Muite Arukou' was titled 'Sukiyaki' in America where it spent three weeks at the top of the Billboard charts, the only song by a Japanese artist to do so. Japanese pop music, or J-pop, followed American influences due to the radio stations playing American music for the troops stationed across Japan. In the 1950s no act was bigger than Elvis and rock music became the thing to listen to. The 60s saw girl groups and boy bands emerge and the 70s introduced electronic music into the scene. J-pop moved away from Western influences in the 80s when electronic keyboards and synthesisers were being developed in Japan, and this influenced the creation of synthpop and citypop. Visual kei changed the rock scene, adding glam-rock inspired crazy hair and flamboyant costumes. X Japan is arguably the country's biggest rock band. Starting in the early 80s as a pioneer of Visual Kei, their second album *Blue Blood* stayed in the Japanese charts for 108 weeks and in their career they've played the Tokyo Dome 18 times.

Idol groups are bands of young people (often women), manufactured by record labels to not only sing and dance, but create a parasocial relationship through merchandise and meet-and-greets. In the 2010s, the idol pop scene grew rapidly leading to the time being dubbed the 'idol warring period' as various groups tried to get fans on their side. The most popular idol group is AKB48, which has over 90 members divided into teams, and holds elections for who will perform on singles. Babymetal is an idol group that performs to metal music. They have played concerts around the world and have had the highest charting Japanese language in the US. The best selling artists currently are the B'z, AKB48, Mr. Children and Ayumi Hamasaki.

A TASTE OF JAPAN

Japan has the most 3-star Michelin restaurants of any country and Tokyo is the city with the most 3-star Michelin restaurants. Sushi, fish served on seasoned rice, has been consumed by the Japanese since the early 19th century and is synonymous with Japanese cuisine. Some Japanese immigrants in the western United States opened restaurants to share their food with the world, but sushi needed a bit of refining to cater to American tastes. The California roll, crab meat with cucumber wrapped in rice, was invented in Los Angeles and helped to introduce Western eaters to the idea of eating raw fish. Perhaps the first time people in the United States even heard of sushi was when Molly Ringwald's character in the 1985 film The Breakfast Club ate some as the other characters looked on confused. There are restaurant chains all over the world now serving sushi that has been adapted for their local tastes as well as the types popular in Japan. Thanks to takeaway apps, ordering sushi is now as common as pizza or Chinese takeaway.

While instant noodles are consumed more in China and India, this quick meal was developed in Japan by Nissin in 1958. Certain brands have managed to become popular worldwide because they are quick to prepare and affordable. One of Japan's largest brands, Cup Noodles had a 60-foot tall sign installed in New York's Times Square in 1996 and the brand is so popular that there is a museum in Yokohama, Japan dedicated to the brand. One of the country's national dishes, curry was introduced to Japan by the British Royal Navy sailing from India in the Meiji era, and it grew in popularity as it was easy to cook large quantities of it at once. Your average curry in Japan is sweeter and less spicy than those from India and is most commonly served with rice and breaded deep-fried pork or chicken. The dish is incredibly popular in the UK, and the term 'katsu curry' is often used when referring to any kind of Japanese curry, even if a katsu cutlet isn't included in the dish.

It is hard to imagine Japan's influence on the world fading any time soon. Those who grew up watching Japanese films or playing video games are at an age where they are having kids of their own and can pass down this interest and introduce it to the next generation at a young age. Foods that were once considered exotic are becoming common, losing that aura of being exotic or unusual but with more people able to enjoy their culinary delights. Japan wields some of the strongest cultural soft power in the world, and you can expect it to produce many more marvels in the years to come.

GOOD FOR NOTHING

EMERGING DURING THE MID-EDO PERIOD, THIS FORMIDABLE CRIME SYNDICATE HAS SURVIVED FOR CENTURIES BY BALANCING TIME-HONOURED TRADITIONS WITH THE NEED TO EVOLVE

To label the Yakuza as 'good for nothing' isn't to insult the largest and most sophisticated criminal organisation that rules from the shadows in a nation of 125 million. It is simply to call them by their name, which originates from a card game (Oicho-Kabu) in which drawing the sequence 8, 9 and 3 (ya-ku-za) is the worst possible outcome – indicating they are not to be messed with.

Founded in the mid-Edo period, this sprawling and complex syndicate began as two gangs – the Tekiya and the Bakuto. The former were peddlers of illicit goods, while the latter focused primarily on running gambling houses. It wasn't until the 19th century that these rivals banded together into a larger, more coherent group that moved into loan sharking, extortion and operating protection rackets. In time, clans (each with their own illegal interests and run by their own head) spread across Japan.

Overseen by a 'father' (the Oyabun), who is in turn supported by a senior advisor and a first and second lieutenant, these clans utilise a pyramid hierarchy, with 'brothers', 'little brothers' and then 'children' below the top tiers, meaning that clans can flourish into enormous 'families'.

Recruits (often working-class people of Korean descent) are required to make a blood oath upon joining. This ceremony is usually conducted inside a Shinto temple and involves the inductee swearing never to betray the group. Doing so can result in a beating, excommunication or being asked to slice off the top of one's little finger as a bloody apology. This particular digit is chosen because it is used to hold the hilt of a sword, thereby its removal makes a man less able to fend for himself and therefore even more reliant on the clan's protection.

Once known for infiltrating the very top of Japanese government (and embroiling a former prime minister in a scandal in which he accepted a $3 million bribe from the US company Lockheed Martin in return for a contract to supply planes in the early 1970s), the Yakuza has since been severely hampered by anti-corruption measures and police crackdowns. Even so, they remain a formidable group, one that has cleverly donated to several emergency relief funds in order to bolster its once waning popularity. With links to criminal networks across Asia and the US, the Yakuza look set to survive for many years to come.

MAIN Although it has numerous illegal interests, the Yakuza also runs legal enterprises, including construction companies, film studios and nightclubs

RIGHT It's common for members of the Yakuza to sport full-body tattoos (irezumi). Administered using sharpened bamboo needles, they can take years to complete

FAR RIGHT By the 1990s the Yakuza had cornered the illegal handgun market and were also making millions from human trafficking

YAKUZA

WHIMSICAL PICTURES

FOR MANY WESTERNERS, THE DISTINCTIVE VISUALS OF MANGA ARE ONE OF THE FIRST THINGS THEY THINK OF IN RELATION TO JAPAN

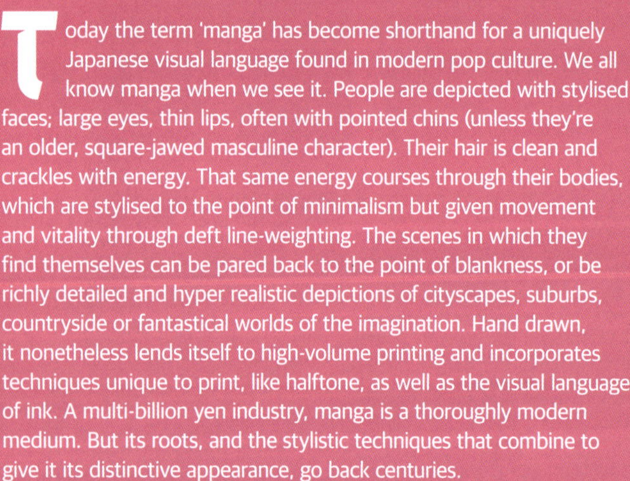

Today the term 'manga' has become shorthand for a uniquely Japanese visual language found in modern pop culture. We all know manga when we see it. People are depicted with stylised faces; large eyes, thin lips, often with pointed chins (unless they're an older, square-jawed masculine character). Their hair is clean and crackles with energy. That same energy courses through their bodies, which are stylised to the point of minimalism but given movement and vitality through deft line-weighting. The scenes in which they find themselves can be pared back to the point of blankness, or be richly detailed and hyper realistic depictions of cityscapes, suburbs, countryside or fantastical worlds of the imagination. Hand drawn, it nonetheless lends itself to high-volume printing and incorporates techniques unique to print, like halftone, as well as the visual language of ink. A multi-billion yen industry, manga is a thoroughly modern medium. But its roots, and the stylistic techniques that combine to give it its distinctive appearance, go back centuries.

The word 'manga' is often translated as 'whimsical pictures' and this is an excellent summation of its origins. A more literal translation could be 'cartoons', in the sense of short, amusing comic strips rather than animation, although the word is sometimes used to describe anime in the UK and US thanks to the 1980s production and distribution company Manga Entertainment (now known as Crunchyroll) which brought many iconic Japanese animated movies and TV shows to western shores.

One of the most famous compilations of these whimsical pictures is the *Hokusai Manga*, a vast collection of sketches by the same Edo period master artist who created the iconic *Great Wave Off Kanagawa* and many other images of Japan's landscapes and everyday life. Hokusai entitled the first volume of his manga collection *Brush Gone Wild* and it started life as a drawing guide before he removed the instructive text and republished it. But manga is older than Hokusai's 19th century works - its roots lie in a type of artwork called emakimono; hand-sized scrolls that are unwound to slowly reveal a visual story. These date back to the 8th century Nara period.

Manga remained a largely Japanese artform until the American Occupation in the wake of World War II. During this period, iconic characters like Astro Boy were created, and introduced to the west by American GIs and their families returning home from occupied Japan or moving onto deployments in Europe. Today manga publishers make up the world's top four comics publishers - massively outstripping western titans Marvel and DC.

MAIN Astro Boy, known in Japan as Mighty Atom and created by Osamu Tezuka in 1952, was one of the first manga characters to become popular outside of Japan

SMALL CIRCLES Manga features stylised and codified features and expressions that are now found in other visual media such as emojis

ABOVE RIGHT This page from the *Hokusai Manga* comically depicts the fortune god Jurōjin and an accompanying lucky rat blessing a small child

MANGA

THE CHRYSANTHEMUM THRONE CONTINUES

WHO IS THE CURRENT EMPEROR OF JAPAN AND WHO COULD SUCCEED HIM IN THE FUTURE?

On December 2017, Akihito announced he would abdicate the throne on 30 April 2019 due to his age and health issues. His oldest son, Naruhito, succeeded him as emperor on 1 May 2019. Born on 23 February 1960, Naruhito graduated from Gakushuin University in 1982 with a degree in history before travelling to Merton College in Oxford, England, where he continued his studies. While abroad he spent time with the British Royal Family and travelled around Europe visiting other royal families from Spain, Norway and Netherlands among others. As crown prince of Japan, Naruhito assumed his father's duties briefly in 2012 when the latter had to recover from heart bypass surgery. Normally the emperor's birthday would be a public holiday in Japan, and as an annual tradition, the emperor makes a public address. However, due to the covid-19 pandemic, public plans for 2020, 2021 and 2022 were all cancelled. Naruhito was finally able to make his first public birthday address as emperor in 2023, for his 63rd birthday.

The name for this new era (or 'gengo'), the Reiwa era, was chosen by a panel and announced shortly after Akihito publicly revealed his plan to abdicate. The name for the new gengo needed to be chosen before Naruhito came to the throne, as it appears on government documents, coins and other official items. The word Reiwa can be interpreted as "beautiful harmony", however, this isn't a direct translation. This is the 248th era in Japanese history and the first to be named from Japanese literature, whereas the names for all previous eras came from classical Chinese texts.

The question of the imperial succession has been an issue in Japan over the last few decades. Emperor Naruhito has one child, Princess Aiko, who is currently ineligible to succeed her father due to a law, passed in 1947, that prevents women from inheriting the throne - even though Japan has previously been ruled by women in their own right. The current heir presumptive is Fumihito, Crown Prince Akishino, Naruhito's younger brother, who in turn will be succeeded by his son, Prince Hisahito. The third and last person currently in line for the succession is Naruhito's 88-year-old uncle, Masahito, Prince Hitachi. With very few male members in the imperial family, the Japanese parliament will likely debate the succession laws for years to come.

MAIN The Japanese royal family, including heir presumptive to the throne Crown Prince Akishino (third from right) wave from the Imperial Palace in Tokyo, 2 January 2023

RIGHT Emperor Naruhito and Empress Masako photographed in May 2019. They were enthroned later that year

FAR RIGHT Emperor Naruhito, Empress Masako and their daughter Princess Aiko. Whether Aiko can succeed the Emperor is still up for debate

THRONE